Making of
Breaking the stigma of addiction

James SHINNy Davenport

Copyright © 2022 James SHINNy Davenport

All rights reserved.

ISBN:

DEDICATION

This book has been dedicated to the still suffering Alcoholic Addicts and the people of the recovery world who continue to pass on a message of experience, strength and hope.

ACKNOWLEDGEMENTS

There's a few people I would like to thank as without them I would have not have had the chance to tell my story. A special mention goes to:

Tony Jones - Writer

Shannon Higham - Puzzle piece insight

Nifty Communications - Management

Everyone in the RECOVERy world that help themselves & others with their daily battles.

"I chose to recover out loud in the hope that others around the world wouldn't suffer in silence."

JAMES SHINNy DAVENPORT

INTRODUCTION

Secrets will keep you sick, just as mine kept me sick for decades. And sick people do sick things. I struggle with my sickness daily, as do millions of other addicts across the world.

It comes as no surprise that the word 'alcohol' is said to originate from the Arabic 'al-khul' which means 'body-eating spirit'. It's a fitting description of alcoholism and addiction in general, which addiction expert Dr Gabor Maté defines as 'any behaviour or substance that a person uses to relieve pain in the short term, but which leads to negative consequences in the long term.' His definition rings perfectly true for me, and I did addiction to the extreme. If it brought me pleasure, I wanted more.

As you might expect, this book tells the story of my downfall into the depths of addiction and my subsequent recovery to the present day, but it also chronicles my journey of how I came to understand addiction – a vital component in long-term recovery success. It's a tale of hope which offers other addicts and their families a chance to understand their afflictions.

It also looks at the behaviours and achievements of those who have found a way to channel their excessive, extreme compulsions into pursuits which are not damaging, often achieving levels of accomplishment and excellence that few regular people can. Using our excessive tendencies in pursuit of good can have astounding results. But, left unchecked and misunderstood, the ease at which addicts can indulge in obscene or damaging pursuits will create mayhem for themselves and everyone around them.

While the stories of my addiction might be thrilling and entertaining to read, it's important to remember that these events were all caused by a disease that almost ended my life and in turn hurt a lot of people. Time and time again I would quit drink and drugs, only to then relapse, each time falling deeper into the chaos and destructive depths of my addiction. Research has shown that stress is the main cause of addictive relapse and behaviour, which again, shines a light on the reasons behind my relapses. If only I knew then what I know now.

Now I know that everything I did was part of my desperation to hide who I was. It was impossible to understand or admit at the time, but I just wanted to stop feeling like a frightened little boy. Because that's what I was, deep down inside – a frightened little boy. To address the problem I needed to revisit the roots of the problem. It took years of work but I got there, in the end.

This book explains how I came to understand exactly what addiction is and how it can be managed and turned to work for us, instead of against us.

Imagine that your body is a car, a vessel that enables you to navigate this thing called life. Let's take a look inside my car and the three men that live there. SHINNy number one is the demonic dude in the back. The pleasure-driven, self-seeking bastard. He is egotistical, self-assured and desires only to get his needs met. He wants more of everything. He is never satisfied and will do whatever it takes to get the job done. Today this guy must never drive the car, he is in the back and is always there watching and waiting for an opportunity to take the steering wheel. He is a master manipulator. He is my addict and if the demonic dude gets to drive, his only destinations will be jails, institutions and death.

SHINNy number two is the passenger. The passenger knows the guy in the back. He also knows the guy who's driving. His job is to mediate between the two. After all, some of the demonic dude's qualities and ideas can be pretty useful. Let's have it right, without him there would be no ink on these pages. We have to listen to what he has to say. He just can't take over completely or we're all fucked and all bets are off… believe me!

SHINNy number three is the spiritual one. He is working out where he is going. He knows the guy in the back is very dangerous, powerful and cunning and he also knows the passenger will try his best to keep him going in the right direction. This SHINNy works a spiritual program. He is a good dad, a respected friend and is unconditionally loved by his family. Only time will tell what is to become of him but I can assure you this, his very own extremism will always be conjuring up some new life adventure.

In this book, after every chapter you will be offered a reflection by soon to be university graduate Shannon Higham. Specialising in psychology she is determined to find out why people become addicted, troubled and violent, exploring nature vs nurture. Shannon and the recovered me will deliver them as pieces of a jigsaw puzzle that will provide you with a perspective and sources of external information for you to explore. It's a key to help people find the path from addiction and despair to recovery, understanding and excellence. If you or someone you know is suffering from addiction, don't hide it. Don't pretend. Understand that you're not alone. There are millions of people in the same position as you.

And if I can do it, maybe you can too.

PART 1.

THE AWAKENING

CHAPTER 1.

HELLO, ARE YOU THERE? ARE YOU READY?

AND SO WE BEGIN

Every addict will, at some point in their life, ask themselves some questions.

How did I end up here? What did I do wrong? Where did it all start?

These questions are not easy to answer, and they're even harder to answer honestly. Few people, least of all addicts, can examine themselves and their life. Few can admit to their mistakes and see the ways they could have acted differently but when we do, something magical happens. The magic is in fact recovery.

That's not to say addicts are entirely to blame for their situations. The World Health Organisation (WHO) has officially described addiction as a disease that centres in the mind of the addict. It seems many addicts were simply bound to be addicts, no matter how good their intentions. In addition, the DMS-IV diagnostic and statistics manual created by American psychiatry lists addiction as a mental health disorder.

I can trace my addiction story back to when I was seven years old.

MAKING OF AN ADDICT

It had been a long day for a seven-year-old, after several hours of playing outside in the quiet side-streets around my nanna's block of high-rise flats. You could do that in the 1980s. Kids could play in the street unsupervised without the fear of social services being called. It was normal back then.

What wasn't normal was what happened next. I was busy with whatever game I was playing at the time when I heard my nanna calling me from the window of her flat. "James! Come in and get a drink! James! JAMES!"

I was certainly thirsty, but the thought of stopping my playtime to climb countless stairs and get a drink didn't appeal to the seven-year-old me. I wanted to carry on having fun, which became something of a lifelong mantra. I was going to have fun. Nothing and no one were going to stand in my way. I knew that I should do as I was told and climb those stairs. My nanna was calling me, and to ignore her went against everything I knew to be right and polite and proper. But still, the idea of stopping my play and climbing those stairs seemed less and less likely the more I thought about it. And soon, a fateful decision was made. Instead of obeying my nanna, I knelt down, bent over and slurped a gulp of dirty water from the puddle which gathered at the bottom of the steps at the base of the flats.

I believe this action was a turning point in my life. It was a lightbulb moment, a surge of energy to my brain which ignited the disease that was waiting within me. It was a turning point which opened a door to let my addiction take control. Drinking from that puddle and disobeying my nanna changed everything. This was the first time I'd given in to a compulsion to do something I knew I shouldn't. Little did I know then but giving into compulsions would become a life-changing habit.

The urge to drink from the puddle was overwhelming (nothing else mattered - I had to have it) but not because I was thirsty. I wasn't dying of thirst and besides, I could get a drink from my nanna, if thirst had been the issue. No, it wasn't thirst which made me drink from the puddle - it was the urge to do something I knew was wrong, the urge to chase pleasure. I knew that drinking the puddle would mean I'd carry on enjoying the pleasures of playtime. It was the compulsion for pleasure that led me to do what I knew I shouldn't, and knowing I shouldn't made it all the more pleasurable.

What the puddle event also did was to convince me that doing the right thing wasn't always necessary, and that doing the wrong thing was sometimes an option. Disobeying nanna was a big deal. She was a scary lady and not doing what I was told would have major consequences but that's exactly what I did, anyhow. Instead of obeying my nanna, instead of recognising that drinking dirty puddles was disgusting and probably risky, I did it anyway, just so that I could continue with the pleasure I craved. I was the boss of my own little world, in that moment I also had control and if doing bad things meant I could have more pleasure, then so be it.

Many addicts say their addiction was ignited by trauma of some kind. For me it was a decision, it was a change in my thinking which subsequently changed my behaviour, making me deceitful, manipulative and chaotic. Addicts know that by rejecting taboos and breaking rules we can experience the pleasures we crave so much. It means we can do as we like and have no constraints on our pleasure-seeking. We can cheat and lie and deceive, and while we won't always get away with it, the pleasure we can experience by ignoring rules and taboos is seemingly worth it to us. We twist the truth in our head to justify our behaviour. We invent ways to make our bad choices acceptable. We create ways to blame others, to make out that the reason we behaved badly was somehow their fault. For us, the truth is not a clearly defined thing. It's something we can manipulate in our minds to justify or excuse our behaviour. Over time, we build a habit of distorting the truth in our minds as a way to continue with our quest for the pleasures our addictions will ruthlessly compel us to crave.

Ok, sure. Half of our brain knows that it's bullshit. Half of our brain manufactures the bullshit, while the other half of our brain buys into it (remember those dudes in the car?) but fuck it. We can easily ignore the inconvenient truth, blinded by the lies we tell ourselves and silenced by the noisy compulsion of our cravings. We buy into our own bullshit. Once you find a way to justify your behaviour to yourself, the consequences are meaningless or at least we'd have ourselves believe that.

MAKING OF AN ADDICT

When I drank from that puddle, I wasn't quenching a thirst.

When I drank from that puddle, I was freeing myself of the constraints of society and opening the door to do whatever the fuck I liked. And what I craved was pleasure, in all its forms.

Looking back, I wish I hadn't drunk from the puddle. I wish I could go back and tell that kid not to do it, because once you excuse yourself from the taboos and society's rules – once you don't care about the truth - all that's left is a craving for more and more pleasure. And the worst part is that you don't give a fuck about the consequences.

Somewhere out there in this universe of infinite possibilities is a young Shinny Davenport who didn't drink from the puddle. There's a Shinny who went upstairs to his nanna's flat and had a drink there instead. I'd love to see how he turned out. But I didn't do that. I drank from the devil's puddle.

And now, here we are. Would I have ended up here anyway? Would it have just been a different story?

PUZZLE PIECE 1

Addictive behaviour was first investigated in the 1930s believing that people with addictive tendencies were morally flawed or lacked basic deterring instincts. Like James said, addiction is now recognised internationally as a chronic disease that impacts both the brain's structure and function.

Addiction eventually hijacks the brain, this happens when the brain goes through a series of awakenings... and this for James was drinking from the puddle, ultimately sparking a recognition of pleasure, pushing him towards compulsive behaviour.

CHAPTER 2.

FEEDING THE DIS/EASE

My first real addiction was food.

From an early age the pursuit of food was a constant feature in my life. It wasn't as if food was in short supply. Unlike many kids from poor families, we always had food on the table and both my mam and my grandparents liked to make sure we were well fed. If anything, I was a little too well fed and a bit porky in my childhood years.

I'd been showing signs of addictive behaviour with food for a long time and I loved anything with a strong flavour. I'd steal vinegar from the kitchen cupboard and hide in a small alcove behind the kitchen door and drink it neat, straight from the bottle. Of course, I knew it was somehow wrong to be drinking vinegar and I knew my mam and my nanna would disapprove. It felt wrong but I'd do it anyway, desperately craving the strong flavour and the mentally distracting kick it gave me.

My sister, Gillian, often had to suffer the consequences of my food addiction as eating more than my fair share became something of a quest. I'd throw my food down my neck as quickly as possible, before trying every trick in the book to get hold of hers too. Shoplifting food from local stores was soon to become a daily routine.

Perhaps the worst example of my compulsion to eat happened when I was eight. Lemon curd sandwiches were a bit of a thing in our house. My grandad would feed me these when I was upset or when I'd been in trouble with my nanna. He'd cuddle me while I cried and make me a 'lemon cheese butty' as we called them. I think my grandad recognised my nanna as a bully, so he'd comfort and console me with food. I knew that he'd give me what I wanted if I asked, so I'd often pester him for food. Food today is still associated with the love and comforts my grandad provided me.

On the day in question, I'd literally filled my face with a lemon cheese butty, my cheeks billowing full of bread as I ran down the steps in my nanna's block of flats. Suddenly, I tripped and fell. I bounced down the steps, hitting my head hard, before landing at the bottom of the stairs. It all happened very quickly, because the next thing I knew I was choking. A neighbour had heard me fall and was thumping me on the back, yelling at me to spit out the food which was lodged in my throat and I remember desperately trying to keep the food in my mouth. Despite my sobs and breathless, choking panic, I still couldn't bring myself to give up the food. Even in this extreme, life-threatening situation, all I could think about was food. It's not the first time my addiction has almost killed me.

Looking back, it seems obvious to me now that I was developing a problem, not only with food, but with my compulsions, cravings and lack of self-control.

More important at the time was the way my addictive behaviours were compounding the very problems that made me behave the way I did. Despite being an active kid, the pure volume of food I was eating caused me to get fat and being fat caused me to get bullied. And, of course, being bullied and being fat made me feel bad about myself and desperate for any pleasures I could find. Which, in turn, caused me to eat more because eating was so pleasurable to me.

Being fat and taunted also made me crave approval. Like most fat kids I felt like a failure. It seemed as if the people I met looked down on me at best and at worst, would ridicule and bully me. I felt left out and wanted nothing more than to be appreciated, cared for and respected. The feeling of worthlessness is something I still haven't fully shaken off and sometimes still clouds my judgement and my life to this day. Craving approval and respect has been a constant feature in my life and is still an issue to some degree - but that's a story for later in the book.

Puzzle piece 2

I believe James' food addiction developed some kind of chemical spark when it came to food; especially food with intense flavours. The addiction can come from not dealing with emotional issues, using food as a coping mechanism mainly when it came to bullying.

It is said that bullying is often the cause and result of all-around trauma in the body and mind which leads to substance abuse and addiction; for James at this point it was food.

Abraham Maslow (1943) proposed a hierarchy of needs. He suggested that in order for a person to feel whole then certain needs must be met. His low self-esteem and emotional damage is evident in this chapter and for James, this was just the beginning of his emotional roller coaster.

CHAPTER 3.

PETE THE BAG AKA MY REAL DAD

I don't call him my dad, because he didn't really fulfil the requirements of the role, but Pete was my biological father. He was also an alcoholic.

As a child I loved the smell of him and I can still recall it today - his Brut, his Old Spice. I adored him for a time and looked up to a man who had an imposing presence, ironically something I am told I have today.

I can't comment on the theories about alcoholism being a genetic condition – I don't know anything about genetics, so it would be daft for me to spout on about something which I clearly know nothing about. What I do know, and I can tell you with some conviction, is that Pete's drinking left a deep and lasting impression on me and helped to form the way I think about drink.

My mam packed Pete's belongings and kicked him out when I was about a year old. He'd been drinking, as was often the case. For some reason I was crying, as one-year-olds often do, much to the annoyance of Pete. When my mam saw him lash out with his foot and kick me, she was shocked, frightened and livid all at the same time. My mam tells me that it shocked her so much she knew he had to leave but I'm guessing there were plenty of other things he'd done previously too. Mam also tells me that Pete never showed me any love, and this is something I remember continuing to be true during the infrequent occasions in later life when we were able to spend time with him.

When I think about Pete and what he was like, a few things spring immediately to mind. The first is that he was horribly bad-tempered. When we were out in public he was always really nice, but when we were alone he'd turn into an unpredictable and angry bastard. Despite us being desperate for his attention and approval, Gillian and I were both scared shitless of his fiery temper. (Incidentally, this is something I recognise in myself to this day.)

The other thing I remember well is the crushing disappointment he often delivered to us. We would see Pete only occasionally and being let down by him was a frequent experience. Gillian and I would eagerly wait for him, watching out of our bedroom window in the hope that he would arrive as promised, but most times we were disappointed. As children this destroyed us. I think any kid would be gutted if their dad thought so little of them that he didn't turn up when he'd promised. And, of course, the less kindness he showed us, the more we needed him to show that he loved us.

Other days, he'd turn up out of nowhere without making any arrangements, whisking us off, quite often to the pub, which brings me on to another thing I remember about Pete.

I recall one time, we were sitting in the pub, each of us kids with a glass of coke and a packet of crisps, watching Pete play pool. Eventually Pete lost, and I could see that he was embarrassed and furious. We recognised the signs, although most people wouldn't see it. We'd seen it all before and I knew the signs well enough to know that he was going to turn into an arsehole. Just the thought of it brings a knot to my stomach but then, something magical seemed to happen. Pete grabbed his drink, took a few big mouthfuls and suddenly, he was okay. It was as if the drink somehow calmed him. He began laughing and joking with his friends. The mood changed and everyone in the pub seemed to enjoy his company. The transformation was astounding.

This calming, happy effect the drink had on him was something which I saw happen time and time again over the years. Whenever something stressful occurred, he'd have a drink. At every happy occasion, he'd have a drink. Wherever he was, whatever the situation, the drink seemed to have a legitimate role to play.

The more time I spent in the pub with Pete, the more the culture and behaviour of 'drinking men' became something I aspired to. Drinking and the accompanying camaraderie seemed to be a big part of being a man, and there was nothing I wanted more than to be liked, looked up to and respected in the same way Pete seemingly was.

Is this not true of society today? Drink is normalised in society and the seed is planted in childhood. Birthdays, Christmas, funerals, stress. Taking your child to get their first legal drink is celebrated. We are taught subconsciously that it's acceptable. Have you ever considered not drinking?

As I grew up, I started going to pubs myself, looking for the same 'manly respect' I'd seen so often during my pub visits with Pete. I'd do the same kind of drinking and showing off I'd seen displayed by many hard-drinking men, and I'd behave just the same to anyone who would watch. I was enthusiastic to please and eager to show my manliness.

I loved the smell of the pub, the noise and the mayhem and, just like it worked for Pete, alcohol became a cure for me too - an answer to any problem I had, the solution to all my woes. Alcohol delivered the pleasure I craved and the confidence I so badly needed. It's no wonder I ended up an alcoholic.

I don't blame Pete. I know he had his own demons to deal with. His father before him was a serious man who showed him no love and Pete hadn't enough courage or confidence to do anything different with me. I know that deep down he had love for me but he had no idea of how to show it. He was lost and confused and I ended up being just the same.

I'm embarrassed to say that I eventually turned into him. Drink made me ignore the things which made me feel bad inside while giving me the confidence to hide my insecurities behind the false confidence which alcohol provided. And drinking offered me an opportunity to be a manly man – just like Pete.

Gillian and I have talked a lot about Pete and we've come out of the other side of this with a clearer understanding of how our childhood experiences with him affected us. Our understanding of those times has caused us to love our own kids in a way that Pete was never able to display with us – and that's one thing we can thank him for, I suppose.

The last time I saw Pete was just a few years ago when he was walking across Salford Precinct. He was obviously not doing well. He was slurring, not focussed and having trouble walking straight, wearing a pair of shorts and long socks with shoes, carrying a tired old bunch of flowers on his way to my sister's place for lunch. He's an alcoholic and I remember thinking, 'You've done me a favour by not being a real dad to me'.

I gave him a lift, largely because I wanted to show him that I was doing okay, that I was sober and had got my shit together. As he got out of the car he said, 'Cheers, Boy'. He always used to call me 'Boy'.

I haven't seen him since; he's dead now anyway.

Puzzle piece 3

A relationship with our father is a powerful bond. For James, this had an enormous, long-lasting influence on his childhood. We wonder if James longed for acceptance in fear of abandonment.

In this chapter, we hear what kind of father James had in his life. Pete was the addicted dad, the distant dad, the absent dad and mainly when he was drunk; the narcissistic dad. All of which left a unique imprint on James' emotions. In turn, we develop anxieties and unconsciously sabotage the things we really want.

CHAPTER 4.

SCH...INNY

Michael was a bully. Not only that but he was also from a family with a mean reputation and even if I stood up to him, there would be consequences. His family were quick to gang up together, so taking on one of them meant taking them all on. Me? I was just a fat, scared kid with a lisp who didn't have any brothers or a dad to protect me. I just hung around with my sister and so I got bullied a lot. Michael was just one of many.

I remember one day when I was about eight years old. Michael was chasing me around a local football field trying to steal my skateboard. I was running away and he was chasing me but I couldn't get away. It seemed to go on for ages and I was terrified. It probably wasn't that bad and likely didn't go on for as long as I remember but at the time I felt like I was running for my life. I was sobbing when I eventually managed to make it home but my problems weren't over. My mam slapped me hard and told me I had to stop being so timid and stand up for myself, because that was the only way to stop bullies from targeting me. It was the last thing I needed. I just wanted to feel safe and loved and, instead, I was made to feel small and worthless again.

She was right, of course, in her own way. But as every scared fat kid with a lisp will tell you, standing up for yourself isn't easy when everyone takes so much pleasure in making your life hell. I felt alone and vulnerable, all the time just wanting to be like the other kids who were seemingly stronger or had the back up to stop themselves being bullied. All I wanted in the whole world was to be liked and respected, rather than bullied and fearful. Most addicts talk about craving as a sense of belonging. The fear and the bullying got so bad that I knew I needed to somehow make it stop. All I could think about was how I could avoid being bullied, and my plan started with getting rid of the lisp.

Even today few people call me James or Jimmy. I've been known as Shinny since my early childhood. The nickname comes from my inability to correctly pronounce 'Jimmy' when I was young. My mispronunciation eventually morphed into 'Shinny' and it stuck. My lisp, along with being fat, became my most recognisable traits and easy targets for other kids to focus on. Kids being kids, they ripped the shit out of me mercilessly. That's just what kids do. The strong ones are affected less than the weaker, more frightened ones and, unfortunately, I was one of the weak, frightened kids. The pain and suffering the bullies caused consumed me.

Eventually my mam took me to get speech therapy and I remember being given homework pronouncing letters and sounds.

"T -T- T."

"S - S - S."

"Tap - Tap - Tap."

I practised for hours but it just didn't seem to help. As soon as I went back to everyday conversations, my lisp returned.

One of the most common traits most addicts share is a compulsive obsession for whatever they set their minds to, especially if the obsession is something which brings some kind of pleasure. Despite the speech therapy not working as I'd hoped, I still became obsessed with getting rid of the lisp, spurred on by the potential pleasure and relief that success might bring. In my room at night, I'd practice saying things without my lisp. If I concentrated hard enough I could do it, but only if I concentrated really hard on talking with the front of my mouth – something which felt entirely unnatural to me at the time.

Eventually, after hours, days, weeks and months of practice, my lisp began to disappear – slowly at first, but with my obsessive focus and determination, I could see progress happening and soon it was all but gone. I think this was the first time I'd used my obsessive behaviour for good, rather than my compulsions causing the usual damage that addicts so often suffer from.

My memories of my childhood are littered with experiences such as this – not so much the determination to overcome obstacles, although this did happen occasionally. My memories are more often of fear and lack of self-worth. I had a lot of fear inside me and I was constantly craving relief from its debilitating, gut-churning effects. I found myself doing anything which offered some relief, anything which helped me to achieve the one thing I craved more than anything - acceptance.

You see, alcoholism isn't exactly craving for alcohol – although of course, there are many ways in which it is. Drug addiction isn't entirely fuelled by the chemical and biological changes the drugs have on the body. Sex addiction, food addiction, drugs and alcohol all work in the same way for an addict. Addiction is a fear-based disease and anything which helps to relieve the fear and alleviate the feeling of worthlessness – that's what addictions are made of. It's the relief from fear and worthlessness we crave, rather than the substance or behaviour itself.

Alcohol takes the fear away and makes you confident, likeable and popular. Sex is a confirmation that someone likes you enough to engage in intercourse and being accepted is a relief from the fear and self-loathing we carry with us always. Food is a pleasure which distracts us from our negative thought patterns by providing some fulfilment. All are a relief from our near-constant state of negative thinking, at least to some degree. But each time we succumb to our compulsions and addictions we are simply lying to ourselves and hiding what we really feel. All the time we're masking the root-cause of our sorrows with distractions but the rewards of these distractions are enough to make us feel worthy, just for a while. Our self-loathing is so heavy that even a temporary, superficial release from the fear which crushes us daily; even a slight relief is, for an addict, compelling beyond anything you could imagine.

And all of this we do to protect the fat, shy, frightened child inside us. That kid needs relief so badly that we'll do anything to numb the fear.

Puzzle piece 4

The psychological impact of bullying is evident, studies have shown children may be prone to physical illness later in life. A 2014 study from researchers at King's College in London, found that negative social, physical and mental health effects of childhood bullies are still evident up to 40 years later.

James' underlying anti-social behaviour relates to his need to belong to particular peers.

Belonging is what shapes children and who they become, belonging acknowledges children's independencies with others and is the basis of relationships according to Childwatch in 2019.

CHAPTER 5.

SEX

By the time I was in my pre-teen years I was already good at manipulating people. I'd lie, cheat and deceive, and I'd use my persuasive skills to get what I wanted. It's been said before that addicts are some of the most ingenious and resourceful people in the world. After all, find me someone who can be homeless, jobless and off their face most of the time but is still able to acquire enough money to buy the necessary drugs or drink to feed their addiction. That takes some doing! And the way we manage it is by being convincingly manipulative. We have transferable skills, we just don't recognise it.

I put this manipulation to work in many different ways, not least in my quest for sex. I'd already become addicted to the euphoria and approval that sex could bring. I was only nine or 10 years old when I built a den on some derelict land called 'The Croft' near my nanna's house. This was where I'd retreat alone to spend hours masturbating with porno mags while gorging myself on food I'd stolen. I'd built the den especially for this seedy purpose. It was somewhere I could retreat to and spend time feeding the demonic dude, chasing the thrills. I knew it would be severely frowned upon if other people found out what I was up to. The den meant I was less likely to get caught.

Speaking of thrills, nothing was more thrilling than the joy rides I would embark on at 14/15 years old. The speed and excitement would rush through my body and stimulate the demonic dude but let's have it right, no excitement would be complete without a good old end result. Yeah, that's right, a wank. The pleasure was so intense and overwhelming that I would have to pull the car over and masturbate.

For most sex addicts. I would imagine that masturbating plays an important role in feeding their addiction, and me, I'm no different. During the times I had discovered whizz I would have, what I now like to call 'whizz wanks'. I would be high and masturbate for hours on end. One wank was never enough just like one drink, one line, one pipe is never enough. It gave me an opportunity to be alone with the disease in my mind and do these things for longer and more often. Again, with addicts, it's always more, more, fucking more.

Once sex and masturbation entered my life, I seemed to be constantly chasing that illicit thrill.

Around this time, I persuaded my babysitter to let me look between her legs and touch her. It took hours to convince her to let me do it, but it then became a regular occurrence once we'd crossed that threshold. Almost as soon as my nanna dropped me off at the babysitter's I'd pester her to let me, and at first, she'd resist, only to eventually relent with the same routine as last time – putting a pillow over her face, which somehow seemed to detach her from the real-life situation she knew should not be happening.

I don't hold the babysitter at all responsible for this situation, which seems so shocking and disgusting today, in retrospect. Even back then, at that age, I had a brain and a persuasive ability far beyond my years. I was not a typical ten-year-old. I looked at my peers as being under-developed as I staged my life doing the things which children far older than me would do, hanging out with older people and getting into the kind of trouble that kids my age should not. Although my babysitter was supposedly in charge, she was not. I was 'mature' beyond my years and she was a victim of my devious manipulations.

MAKING OF AN ADDICT

Sex is extremely compelling for addicts and it is a difficult addiction to control. Sex is usually free and the consequences can be just as catastrophic than the obvious problems that alcohol and drugs can cause. Sexually transmitted diseases, feeding the seedy sex industry and ultimately breaking up families. Sex is such a great ego boost that we fearful and weak addicts will do whatever it takes to chase that reassuring rush. When someone compliments us by giving us that kind of attention, our addiction is all over it. We crave the self-assurance, the worship, the achievement and the accolade.

From my early teens on I became a good-looking cunt and every girl in Salford wanted a piece of me and yeah, they got it! They wanted the association of being on my arm and I just wanted a fuck. When I became addicted to crack, I would hang out in crank dens.

In crack houses I was treated like a God. I had money and drugs unlimited which in turn meant getting blow jobs on tap. I was a crack king.

I needed people to love me and would do anything to get it. There is still some truth in that today.

Puzzle piece 5

Sex addiction is often connected to traumatic childhood experiences. For James, this was attachment-related trauma that continues to affect his ability to form healthy relationships. James' parental issues were connected to neglect, leaving him feeling vulnerable and unworthy of affection.

However, childhood trauma is not always connected to this. Drug abuse from an early age can develop sex addiction and James uses this as a substitute in search of acceptance. Once the addiction started, it dominated James, substituting one thing for another.

CHAPTER 6.

FEAR ME OR RESPECT ME... THE CHOICE IS YOURS

Overcoming my lisp and becoming sexually active were catalysts for a major change in me. My outward confidence had grown as a result and I went from being bullied to becoming the bully. I say 'outward' confidence because, inside, I was still a frightened child. However, I'd learned that manipulating and frightening people was a way to avoid being picked on. Of course, the fear was still there, inside, and my behaviour was just a smokescreen to avoid that which I was most frightened of – humiliation. A feeling I knew all too well.

At junior school I was a terror. I had an old head on my shoulders and could outwit most kids, and some of the adults too. Although I hadn't had many fights, I was the cock of the school. I craved to be the centre of attention and did what I needed to do to build a reputation as someone not to be fucked with. I knew that the other kids would be frightened of me if I was naughty, so I did naughty things for attention and for the notoriety it brought me. I'd act up, play the role of a tough, naughty kid, and used the threat of my older cousin to scare anyone who tried it on with me. I too felt scared, I hadn't changed inside but blagging kept me safe.

When I eventually went to high school I soon realised I was no longer the toughest kid there and that I would need a new strategy if I was going to avoid being bullied. On my first day I watched a lad called Gary Glendenning batter a kid who was two years older than him. Gary was massive for his age and I was shit scared of him. Instinctively I knew the best thing to do would be to make him a friend.

Gary and I started smoking weed together when we were about 13. A nearby neighbourhood was notorious for drug dealing and we'd often go there to pick up a 'fiver's of weed'. Looking back, I can see that it was almost inevitable that I'd get into drugs. As an addict, anything which provides pleasure is jumped upon, regardless of how wrong, immoral or illegal it is. And not only were drugs rife in the Salford area of Manchester where I lived, but the people who were involved with drugs were the type of men that nobody messed with. It's no wonder drugs held such an allure to me.

In the early years of high school, I was still pretty fat but by the time I reached 14 I was already a regular at the gym. It all started because I was fascinated with bodybuilders. The 1990s was the golden era of bodybuilding and I regarded the champion bodybuilders of the day as gods. I remember seeing Dorian Yates, the Mr Olympia of the day, in magazines and thinking that nobody in their right mind would mess with him.

One Christmas I'd been given some weights which I had been using obsessively, even though I didn't know what I was doing. One winter's evening, after I'd been training for a while in my bedroom, I began flexing my imaginary muscles, posing and examining myself in the reflection in my bedroom window. What I didn't realise was, outside in the street, there was a gang of local lads bent double with laughter as they watched me pose and flex. One of them, Mike, was someone I knew. He managed a local bodybuilding gym and he said that I could train there for free whenever I liked. The gym was my idea of heaven. I loved the vibe, the smell, the noise and the people. Almost everyone there was big, powerful and scary – exactly what I wished to be.

There's nothing wrong with working out and getting fit. There's nothing wrong with building a body you can be proud of. There's a discipline required of anyone who does this, and these are traits which would be of great benefit to normal people. But for addicts, bodybuilding is just another thing to become compulsive about. For anyone like me who had yet to deal with their low self-worth and vulnerability, becoming big and scary at the gym is an obvious way to cop-out. Instead of dealing with the issues which afflict us on the inside, we can dedicate ourselves to creating an exterior image which means few people will want to fuck with you.

While this might seem like a great solution at the time, the underlying fear and vulnerability are still there. Only now, you're playing a much more dangerous game. Now you're solving your problem with the threat of violence. Instead of earning respect because of who you are, your 'respect' is achieved because people are scared of you. Except, it's not really respect, of course, but fear. But if people fear you, they'll not try to humiliate you, and that's all we want. If they don't really know you then it doesn't matter if they don't like you. Being feared is not the same as being respected, but the results are similar enough and attractive enough for us to want it all the more.

Within weeks of starting training at the gym I was taking steroids. If I was aggressive and badly behaved before, it was nothing compared with where I was headed. Looking back, the last thing the world needed was a bigger, stronger version of frightened and angry Shinny.

Puzzle piece 6

Alexandra Hua once said, children victimised are more likely to exhibit aggressive behaviours towards others. This phenomenon may lead to a vicious cycle whereby bullies create bullies out of those they victimise.

Although James became an easy target in school the change in his social behaviour became a risk factor. In order for James to be accepted and dominant he felt the only way to become all these things was to become a bully; a continuous front that would later carry on in adulthood rendering him psychologically and socially vulnerable.

CHAPTER 7.

AHEAD OF THE GAME

I'm surprised when I see people's reactions when I tell them I was taking drugs before I was a teenager. As it turns out, my experience is not typical and even the most unruly kids don't start taking drugs until they get to their later high-school years. In my world, it seemed like almost everyone I knew was drinking, smoking and taking drugs much earlier than that.

My drinking started really early. My grandad would let me sip his Newcastle Brown Ale when I was about seven years old, and my visits to the pub with Pete had a strong effect on me. Watching him socialising and becoming more likeable made me want to drink too. I wanted to be like him, a grown-up man, so I'd try to get hold of alcohol any way I could.

Smoking cigarettes was as natural as breathing for most of us from a really early age. Kids would steal singles from their smoker parents and some of us would chip in together to buy a pack of ten from the local corner shop. We'd often have to get someone to buy them for us but there was always someone willing to do so.

By the time we were old enough to go to high school we were sniffing Tippex and aerosols. Drinking booze was commonplace, as was smoking weed, which we bought from the local dealers in 'fivers' - small strips of cannabis resin. Despite the fact that weed made me throw up the first time, and also made me paranoid pretty consistently thereafter, I was still compelled to smoke at every available opportunity. I didn't like it much, but it made me look cool and made me part of the bad-boy gang. Typically, I had to go one step further than everyone else. And, by the time I was 14, I was selling weed to my fellow school kids.

The first time I did LSD was a major turning point in my journey to addiction. Cigarettes, weed, alcohol and even amphetamines (which we called whizz) were common occurrences at that age, but I was always looking for the next big thrill. I was always ready to take the next step and do the thing which was bigger, badder or stronger than the last – and it came in the form of LSD. A friend from school had managed to score a couple of acid tabs which we took at lunchtime between classes. Needless to say, the drug knocked my brain sideways and the world would never be the same again. From then on, I would take acid as often as I could get hold of it, indulging in the mind-altering worlds which took me on wild adventures far away from my uncomfortable real-life reality.

When drugs are so widespread and acceptable from such an early age it is no wonder that kids will try to experiment with them. The question is, why do some of us go on to be addicts, while others do not? It's a question scientists have no answers for, but there's obviously something about addicts which makes them more susceptible to addiction. Otherwise, every kid from my youth would be fucked up and addicted – and they're not. So, why me?

Puzzle piece 7

James continues to ask why he became an addict and others do not. This depends on the person. A combination of factors in the person influence the risk of addiction.

Three categories for these risks are: our biology, environment and development.

For James, biology definitely seems to fit, with his father also being an alcoholic, it is possible he could have inherited addiction through mental health diseases and disorders.

James was surrounded by drugs and alcohol from an early age whether that be for acceptance or economic status. A person's environment can affect them greatly from peer pressures, physical abuse, early exposure to drugs and lack of parental guidance.

Finally, James' early drug-taking has likely affected his development. Drug use at any age can become addictive. however the earlier it begins the more likely it is to continue. This would have been problematic in his teen years as his brain would have still been developing.

CHAPTER 8.

CALCULATED VIOLENCE

By the time I'd left school violence was a big part of my life, but even before then, I was already acting in a way which was unpredictable and disproportionately violent. I say 'disproportionately' because even though violence itself is awful enough, I often seemed to go overboard, inflicting more pain than necessary and being violent when it wasn't at all called for. Like all addicts, moderation wasn't something I was good at.

I'd been hanging around with older kids since I went to high school but by the age of 15, I was a regular at the gym and was hanging around with adults – many of whom seemed to be living a life which was, let's say, less than angelic. The gym regulars included a decent smattering of gangsters and drug dealers and most of these would eventually become friends of mine.

It's not surprising that training and steroid abuse enabled me to get big quickly, but what is surprising is that I also became freakishly fast. Take those two attributes, couple them with my naturally aggressive nature and you can see why I got picked for the school rugby team.

Mr Preston was my high-school PE teacher and school rugby

coach, and he hated me – especially the tattoo I had on my shoulder of a cannabis leaf, with the words 'Smoke it!' beneath. Like all the teachers at school, he considered me a troublemaker, but Mr Preston could also see I would be useful on the rugby field.

I remember an incident during a school rugby tournament when we were facing one of our big rival teams. The captain of the opposing side was a kid called Kirk, who also happened to be the cock of the rival school with a notorious reputation as a tough guy. This was, of course, like a red rag to a bull for me. At one point during the match, I took Kirk down, quite legally I should add, but he was not happy about it at all. The resulting fight ended up with me being sent off. As I made my way toward the changing rooms, I walked past Mr Preston, and he could see I was absolutely fuming.

"I'm going to fucking kill him!" I muttered as I walked past.

"No, you're not," replied Mr Preston. "You're going to get changed and calm down."

To which I simply replied, "Nah! Fuck that!"

With my boots in my hand, I walked onto the pitch and straight toward Kirk. The match was still underway but by this point I didn't give a fuck about anything. All I could think about was revenge. I could hear Mr Preston screaming at me to stop, but I'd already lost my mind and was completely focused on the task in hand. As I reached Kirk, he looked round at me, just in time to see me swing the boots with all the strength I had to smack him squarely in the face. It was a perfect hit. The sound of the strike echoed across the field and Kirk went down like a sack of shit, bleeding from a sizeable gash above his eye. As he lay on the ground clutching his face, I stood over him, screaming at him to, "Stay down, or I'll fucking kill ya!" – and I think I really fucking meant it.

There were plenty of other violent and unnecessary occasions during my high-school years. It was during this time when violence became my primary setting, not only to deal with the inevitable challenges from other kids but also in a pre-meditated attempt to develop my reputation as a hard man – someone who could be unpredictably violent, simply because he enjoyed it. I kicked a door hard so that it smacked against the head of a teacher as he bent down to pick something up, just for a laugh. I pushed a kid out of a second-floor window as he sat on the sill chatting with his friends, just for a laugh. I drove a motorbike across the rugby pitch while a game was in progress. I stole a car and drove it to school for weeks. I drank beer and took LSD during school. It all added to my notoriety and celebrity, and fed a need to be adored, validated.

I did so many violent and abhorrent acts, just for laughs and to perpetuate my reputation, all to shed the stomach-wrenching feeling of worthlessness that plagued me constantly. Showing off and being violent was my way of avoiding humiliation and defeat. The frightened little boy inside me simply couldn't handle people making him look small, so I worked out a way to avoid these afflictions at any cost. It's called a little Einstein and related to "life scripts" in TA therapy (Transactional Analysis).

I wish I'd had a mentor to help me to properly process the feelings

I had inside me, the hurt and the anger caused by the bullying and my absent father's betrayals. I wish I'd realised I could avoid feeling small and insignificant, simply by understanding myself and the world around me a little better. I wish I'd had that guidance, but I didn't.

Instead, my compulsive and addictive behaviour provided me with a different option. Instead of undertaking the long and difficult process of working through my insecurities, I threw my heart and soul into building a reputation as a hard man that should not be fucked with. And in doing so, fewer people would be brave enough to bully or intimidate me, and those who did could be made to pay the price. I knew my behaviour, my violence, was wrong, but I felt powerless to stop it. The relief and pleasure I got from acting this way were enormously compelling and addictive to the lost soul inside me looking for relief. It looked and felt like respect although, in reality, it was simply fear.

But at the time it seemed like a perfect solution. All of the male role models that I looked up to were big, hard men that no one would dare to challenge. They didn't have to worry about people making them look small or stupid. They didn't allow people to treat them badly. They demanded respect, and they got it.

What I didn't realise at the time is that, almost inevitably, the hard man image is just a front. It's a thin and fragile veneer that we use to protect our delicate egos from harm. The hard man behaviour I saw in films didn't work out so well in real life, because there are real-life consequences for acting violently. The choreographed fights you see on TV are nothing like the dirty, embarrassing, horrific brawls that happen in real life, which make people scream and run away in terror. Normal people aren't impressed by violence, and I was not the justice- administering super-hero I imagined myself to be in my head.

Instead, I was just a little boy, terrified of being bullied, looking small and feeling insignificant. Instead, I built my body and my hard man reputation. I demanded respect in the hope that I'd never have to face humiliation. But, as I said, real life just doesn't work like that.

PUZZLE PIECE 8

James shows early signs of rage and hate, particularly towards males. The fight on the rugby field could have been to state his authority, or a result of envy to people that seemed to 'have it all'.

For James' violence offered a short escape from the hate he already felt; a temporary relief. Having older friends at the gym gained him love and acceptance that was non-existent in his absent father. The violence made him feel free from the typical social hierarchy, knowing he wasn't abiding by the normal restraints of the people that deemed him a troublemaker or problem child.

The internal conflict he had between his ID, ego and superego, lead to his irrational behaviours and later on his addiction. Eventually, James needed a social identity in order to gain self-esteem and respect, not only from individuals but also from himself. James fuelled himself into the mechanisms of social identification in order to adopt the identity and behaviour of the group he was in.

The violence may have been a result of PTSD from being bullied as a child, which is known as an aftershock in his upcoming teen years. It may also stem from cognitive problems of self-expression known as intellectual impairment, which can manifest aggression.

James may have had difficulty with anxiety and frustration, and as a result, he fails to verbalise his feelings, which can cause aggression and impulsivity.

Lastly, he could have been using violence as a form of an adrenaline rush. This violence may have been meaningless and just a form of expression in the only way he knew to be understood, seen and respected. Was that childhood anger and violence the beginning of his addiction to the adrenaline rush?

CHAPTER 9.

A MOTHER'S LOVE

By the time I was 15 I wasn't frightened of anybody – except my mam. Despite how big and mean and tough I was, my mam still held a terrifying power over me, and I would do anything to avoid upsetting or disappointing her. My youth seemed to have been spent in constant dread of being grounded, which was the ultimate punishment for a street kid like me.

Somehow, I only ever brought trouble to her door a couple of times. When I was 13, I smashed a car window with a crowbar. I can't remember why I did it, but the police came to the house and questioned me about it. Of course, mam was devastated. When she asked me why I did it I told her I heard voices telling me to do bad things, knowing that, by lying, I'd have a chance of being let off. The lie got me a weekly meeting with the school psychologist and, while I'd like to say that the shrink somehow understood me and managed to help me in some way, the meetings were just a pile of shit. It was a waste of time and I don't remember it being a significant experience in the slightest. The psychologist tried his hardest, but all I remember was the ways that I tried to outsmart that fucker. Looking back, I seem to have managed to do a good job of it too!

Although I didn't bring the police to the door, I was always in some kind of bother or another, and I must have been a fucking nightmare for my mam. It's likely that mam didn't want to get too involved with my life outside the house, knowing darned well she'd find out things she'd rather not know. To be honest, she probably had enough on her plate trying to put food on the table and keeping the show on the road. She worked a handful of low paid jobs, cleaning offices and the like, and I know she worked her ass off, with long hours and shifts all over the place. The last thing she needed was some little arsehole like me bringing her more shit to deal with.

Despite my increasingly bad behaviour and errant ways, my mam was always the one person in my life that I knew I could rely on. Yes, I was a fucking nightmare, but I was the apple of her eye and she rarely lost her shit with me. In turn, the idea of upsetting her or making her angry was the last thing I wanted to do. As a result, I tried my best to shield her from the stuff I got up to when I was out of the house. I would routinely lie when I got caught out. My manipulative tendencies came into their own when I had to explain things to my mam, and I'd present the story in a way which somehow made me look like the innocent victim, or at least made it look like my behaviour wasn't as bad as it really was. And, thankfully, she'd seemingly believe me. Or perhaps she didn't and just let me off anyway. Either way, whatever I did, whatever I got up to, she would blindly have my back.

Somehow, through all of it, she continued to love me and was always on my side. Even to this day, despite everything I have put her through, she describes me as a 'loveable rogue' and "a good kid, but he's got a bit of a temper". I wish that was the extent of it.

In truth, however, I was an unpredictable, violent, drug-dealing addict who was rolling with an increasingly bad crowd. At school my mates were mostly rough lads who liked a fight and a drink but by the time I'd left school the people around me were serious criminals.

Puzzle piece 9

As we hear in chapter 9 James expresses trust and respect in his mother and highlights how he wanted to deter any trouble from her door. Although James had a very perfect front at home, in social settings he became another person. He seemed to have a mixture of emotions built up and kept them from his mother, as he didn't feel she could tolerate him as he truly was.

James was often labelled as a naughty child, however, in psychological terms, this could be just an early sign of the exploration of his authenticity and independence. From an early age, his lying and manipulative behaviour was a way of accessing his logical brain to get his own way, and as you can tell, this worked.

James' mum worked multiple jobs in order to provide, and as a result, she became over-stimulated. This in turn caused a cumulative stress reaction with James and he would therefore spend less time with her. This relationship could have also added to psychological stress as a young adult.

He regularly surrounded himself with persistent offenders in the violence and drug scene and this tampered with the innocence of his emotional and physical development. Although James seemed to have an unsympathetic demeanour and deemed himself in control of any situation, in reality, he was vulnerable and his psychological risk factors as an adolescent became exposed.

CHAPTER 10.

New friends

Not many school leavers make the kind of money I did at 16. Then again, not many school leavers have a thriving business dealing drugs. I was selling mostly whizz (amphetamines), but also dabbled a bit in weed and, occasionally, coke. I was moving a couple of ounces of whizz each week, making about £600 – that's £2400 a month. For a seventeen-year-old, in the early 1990s, that was a lot of money.

Two brothers were members at the gym where I trained. While I already had some idea that they weren't exactly law-abiding citizens, when I found out the extent of their 'business interests' I was in awe.

For a kid like me who looked up to big, successful hard men with money, the brothers were exactly the kind of people I wanted to be around. Eventually we became mates and they gave me a 'half bar' of whizz to sell – 4.5 ounces. Of course, my usual dealer didn't like it and, for most people this defection could have caused some trouble. But, for some reason, I got away with it and they became friends and business associates and, from there, I could more or less do whatever I wanted.

By then I already had a reputation as a local hard man but my association with the brothers pushed my status up a few notches.

These guys, and the people they hung around with, were everything I wanted to be – all flash cars and gold chains, tough-guy drug dealers who could do what they liked and were frightened of no one. I spent my time working my way into the inner circles of Salford's drug-dealing gangster scene and, even though I was far younger than everyone else, I was manipulative enough and crazy enough to hold my own.

By this point I was making well over a grand a week, easily, and I was spending money like water. I remember one day I had almost

£10K hidden in boxes under my bed – and this was the early 1990s, remember.

Although my reputation and my profile were in another league, the frequent violence and drug-taking, which had been a regular feature of my youth, wasn't so much of a problem at this point. It had reached the point where people just didn't fuck with me, either because they knew who I was, or simply because I looked like I was going to eat your fucking spleen. In fact, I was often able to diffuse troubles which were brewing out of control. People knew that I was connected and that trouble needed to be cooled if they didn't want a fucking nightmare to turn up at their door. Even debt collection was pretty peaceful because people knew that if it turned nasty, it was going to get very fucking nasty indeed. As is often the case in nature, the art of intimidation will often avoid the need to actually fight. It's a good thing because you didn't want to be fighting with the people I had around me.

When things did get violent it was always with someone who didn't know what they were getting themselves into. I've always found it interesting to see how people who are not used to being around serious violence seem to be far too brave for their own good. It's as if they are so sheltered they have no clue about just how bad things could get. It's one of the reasons why people say, 'It's the quiet ones you have to watch'. Most people who know how to fight will do as much as they can to avoid it, because they know that if shit goes off, it has the potential to be really bad. These are the people who will only resort to violence when it is necessary.

By that token, I shouldn't have cared less about the gobby dickheads in nightclubs but my ego would invariably stop me from walking away. It's hard to turn your back when you know you can't lose. The people I had around me meant I never had to worry about that, and so I could always, 'Teach the gobby dickhead a lesson'. Or at least, that's what I thought I was doing. To be honest, I wasn't interested in hurting them though. All I wanted was for them to show me some respect, and that meant I had to belittle them in any way I could. With my reputation and the backup I had, making people show their respect was pretty easy – even if that respect was, in truth, fear.

Some of the people I was hanging around with had been involved in some pretty serious shit – kidnapping, shootings, knife violence and plenty of other stuff too. By association many folk thought I did the same, but I didn't ever get to that stage. I was simply leeching off my gangster-friends' notoriety. I rarely had to live up to that reputation, but I wanted the same respect.

The slowdown in drug abuse was even more interesting and ironic. On the one hand I was obsessive about bodybuilding, exercise, nutrition and, to some degree, health. From Monday to Friday, I was dedicated to the cause, training every day and eating right. But at the weekend I would party to excess. I was the party boy. I was the hard man. I was the sex fiend. And I wanted as much of those things as I could get. When your party was winding down in the early hours, I was just getting started. I'd drink until I was drunk, and then I'd go out to the club and drink some more. And all through the evening and the morning thereafter, I'd be sniffing fat mounds of coke up my nose.

The stupidity of my two lives was entirely lost on me at the time, but in retrospect I understand why it came to be that way. To the untrained eye I was inconsistent, fucking up all of the hard work I'd done during the week with my debauchery at the weekend. But that's only what you can see on the surface. Underneath I was simply feeding my addictions 24/7. I was addicted to working out, to feed my ego and to maintain the defences I'd put in place to avoid being bullied. I was addicted to power as an antidote to the helplessness and weakness I felt eating away at me inside. I was addicted to drink and drugs, because it took away the pain for a while and made me feel like

I was confident, likeable and worthy. And I was addicted to the party life, which was the ultimate reassurance that I wasn't a loser. All in all, these things made me feel like I was somebody, and that was all I ever wanted.

PUZZLE PIECE 10

As a 17-year-old boy James' life became drastically more dangerous, which fuelled his social identity and the need to be liked by the no-good figures that lingered over him. James' social comparison was fed by ego. In basic terms, he evaluated groups based on power and status; figuring out what he could get from them rather than what they could get from a vulnerable teenager with anger issues.

Maintaining the social status of the drug world became important to him, feeding his ego and filling an emptiness within. He couldn't bear the thought of losing this status and would do anything to keep it, whether it be good or bad.

This is where we begin to meet the three stages of James, the ID, ego and superego, all mentioned in previous chapters.

While in this chapter we hear of his ego evolving, it is his superego where the real trouble begins.

CHAPTER 11.

The Hacienda Days

Holly and I had been together since we were 15 years old, having met at a local hangout called Langworthy Road. We got on like a house on fire, almost literally. She was gorgeous, as well as being a tough lass from a renowned local family - her dad, brothers and cousins all being well known in the area as people you should not mess with.

She was my first love, my soulmate at the time I guess, but our relationship was explosive from the start – a meeting of two kindred spirits. Holly was well fit. Blonde curly hair, always looked the part and to top it off she was one seriously crazy bitch who would be happy to fight anyone, and she often did, even knocking out blokes that got on her wrong side.

Predictably, Holly and I would always be getting into fights, both with each other and with other people. Fighting other people was brilliant because I knew she could handle herself and I didn't have to worry about her. Fighting between ourselves was a nightmare because we were both so mental we would always go over the top, take things too far and cause damage that would end most relationships. However, for us, fighting was simply part of our normal daily life, and we both got a buzz from the drama. We were as bad as each other.

By the time I was 17, Holly and I were well known on the Manchester nightclub and music scene. I was already hanging around with some of the City's most notorious gangsters, dealing drugs and building a reputation as a hard man. Although we weren't legally old enough to go, we were regular faces at the popular Hacienda during the height of the late 1990s dance and rave scene.

I was essentially untouchable in there, largely due to the people I hung around with, and I behaved with an arrogance that often led to fights. I'd kick open toilet cubicle doors if I heard anyone sniffing drugs and relieve them of their stash for me to enjoy later. But I'd also get into fights because of my drug-fuelled paranoia. I went from 0-100 very quickly, even with people I knew well. I often thought that people were staring at me, plotting to kill me, when in fact, they were most likely looking at me warily, knowing that I was the local maniac.

My nights out with Holly were equally volatile, with our fall-outs being legendary, frequent and invariably made worse by my cocaine-induced paranoia. By this time I was taking shit loads of coke and, despite her best efforts, there was no way for Holly to avoid my paranoid wrath. I'd watch her behaviour, looking for the slightest indication that she was being disloyal. I'd kick off if I caught her speaking to other people, even if they were a member of her family, and I was convinced that she was shagging people behind my back, even though it was me who was the cheat.

And then, when my paranoia reached its peak, a fight would ensue with whoever had seemingly crossed me. The strange thing is, Holly would always be there to back me up, kicking and punching our supposed enemies until, inevitably, the fight was won. Despite our rows, and my wholly unacceptable behaviour and my unreasonable expectations of her, she was still always there for me, on my side and backing me up, no matter what. In the normal, wholesome, non-violent world in which most people live, no sane soul would want to be with someone as volatile and destructive as me. But there Holly was. By my side, every time.

I remember once being in my bedroom at my mam's with Holly, high as fuck, twisted and paranoid on coke. Somehow I'd convinced myself that there were people in the garden who were out to get me.

This was the middle of winter – it was dark and there was snow on the ground, but I was certain that I was going to be attacked. I ran out into the garden in my boxers with a screwdriver and an axe, ready to fight. Finding nobody there, I still couldn't be convinced that there was no danger, despite my mam and Holly panicking, trying to get me back in the house. At the time, my dad worked for a taxi firm, so I called the taxi base and gave the 'dynamite' codeword which signalled that we were being attacked. Minutes later a dozen or so cabs turned up at our house, looking for the trouble I'd told them we were in. Mum and Holly had to explain the situation away, telling the lads that I had lost my head. My coke paranoia often created situations such as this.

I sound like I was a nightmare, and while that's true, in many ways Holly was just as bad. In our frequent arguments we'd often come to blows, and it was Holly starting it just as often as it was me. While I didn't hit her with punches like I would if I was fighting a bloke, hair pulling and slapping were commonplace.

I remember one occasion when I was getting ready to go out for the evening, probably on my way to meet some lass behind Holly's back. I guess Holly knew this and, although she couldn't prove I was up to no good, she was rightfully suspicious and jealous and so she did her best to stop me from leaving. The usual fight kicked off with both of us pushing and shoving, slapping and punching, screaming blue murder at each other before, eventually, I managed to get away and jumped in my car.

By this point I'd already lost my mind to rage. As I started the engine and dipped the clutch I caught sight of Holly leaping in front of the car in an attempt to stop me. Next thing I knew, the car leapt forward, knocking Holly off her feet to disappear under the bonnet. Thankfully, the wheels didn't go over her and she was okay, apart from a few scrapes and bruises. It frightened the shit out of us both because we know how easy it would have been for her to have died that night.

You might wonder how I got away with this when Holly's family were not shy about kicking people's heads in if they thought they deserved it, and I certainly did. Typically for me, and it's true for many addicts, I'd already consider the situation and, thanks to my habitually manipulative behaviour, I'd managed to hedge against it ever happening. Right at the beginning of the relationship I'd gone to meet Holly's parents and befriended them, making good friends with her mum. I did my best to charm her and make her like me, knowing that this would likely help if the men in the family ever took a dislike to me. Holly's mum and I got on well, and I still think the world of her today. Amazingly, after all I put her through, I'm still mates with Holly and her brothers too.

Despite our fighting, Holly and I had an unbelievably strong bond. We felt like we were untouchable partners in crime who were destined to be together, no matter what. But despite all this, my ego would not let me value our relationship enough to stop me fucking other girls. Okay, so Holly and I weren't perfect, but I wasn't shagging around with a plan to find someone better. I was just shagging around because I could.

I can see why it was so easy for me to get women back then, and I hope this doesn't come across as being too boastful, but I was a good-looking chap with a great body honed by hours in the gym, and I was successful with plenty of money to throw around. Plus, I was a hard-man too. I guess I was the typical alpha male, and for many women, that's attractive. For me, the addict, all I ever wanted was the adoration of other people, so when girls gave me the slightest hint that they were interested, I knew I had to fuck them. I just couldn't say no to the attention because it was just as alluring as a class A.

Somehow, I managed to keep my shagging around from Holly, or at least I think I did. In the beginning we were solid, but after a few years it was obvious that we could never have worked, despite the fact that at the time we felt like we were strong and we were meant to be together. We thought we could make something of it. We had a deep connection that deserved more respect than I could ever give.

Puzzle piece 11

As an impressionable young adult, adolescence and early adulthood are critical periods to establish healthy behaviour. James' environmental determinants began in the gym with the older crowd, maintaining the front of drugs, violence and anger, which originally started off as a defence mechanism, before slowly creeping into relationships.

In order to get his own way, he used his overwhelming anger and manipulation. In 2016 a study showed that out of 55 subjects 53% reported paranoid delusions and auditory hallucinations from cocaine-induced psychotic symptoms; delusions are in fact likely to be related to a schizophrenic process. Adding to the already highly fuelled relationship that was James and Holly, his manipulative ways had taken place once again. James' lack of self-esteem fuelled his anger and paranoia with Holly and his obsessive ways stemmed from his own actions of infidelity, and not even this soul mate could come between his ego addiction and the urge to be in the social spotlight.

CHAPTER 12.

A NIGHT OUT WITH 'BIG SHIN'

We would start drinking around 6pm. My reputation as a maniac was already established at this point. The people I hung around with were wild enough by most people's standards, but I was always the worst, the most extreme. It was always me who would push it to another level.

Of course, I looked like a hard man in those days. I was training at my friend's bodybuilding gym and taking every steroid and performance- enhancing drug going – Dianabol, Deca and Nap 50s, plus whatever else I could get my hands on. As with most things, I didn't moderate my training or my steroid abuse. I was training five days a week and taking more than the recommended dose of the drugs. You were supposed to take 50ml of Nap 50s each day. I was taking five times that amount. With me, it was always more, more, fucking more.

The big night out started in our local, The Woolpack in Salford. At that time drinking wasn't a daily thing with me, not like it would become later. Ironically, I spent the weekdays honing my body to be a finely tuned athletic machine (let's ignore the drugs for now, eh?), but my weekends were spent getting wasted. With this weekend being my 18th birthday bash, it was accepted by all involved that it was going to be a messy one.

I'd been selling drugs for a few years by this point, so my supply for the night was pretty big. Over the preceding years I'd gone from smoking weed to dealing whizz and then, eventually, cocaine. I'd also gone from being a recreational cocaine user to being a greedy one. A gram of coke might be a good night out for most people. For me, it would be at least a quarter of an ounce, and more likely a half-ounce on a big night like tonight. I wasn't a fancy coke sniffer either, cutting neat lines to snort. Not me. I'd tip big piles of it onto my hand and get as much up my nose as I could, before returning to the bar for another drink, usually Murphy's or Guinness – not that cheap lager piss that most blokes drink. And that's how the evening would begin, down a pint then nip to the bogs for a sniff, often dragging some bird with me for a quick shag in exchange for a line or two. Sounds like a real laugh, doesn't it? Like in a film or something.

To be honest, even talking about this now gives me a bit of a buzz. It's a thrill that addicts call 'euphoric recall'. I'm remembering the pleasure, the abandonment of responsibility and the wild buzz. I remember feeling like I could do anything I wanted and nobody would, or could, do anything to stop me. It's something which addicts have to deal with every day of our lives, fighting the urge to enjoy those thrills again. I can't tell you how fucking difficult it is to resist those urges. Only an addict will understand. Sitting here now, there's nothing I'd like more than to be back there living it up and not giving a single fuck about anyone or anything.

Thankfully I'm older and wiser now with the experience and learning behind me to know that those behaviours have consequences, and that, one day, I'd have to pay for it all. And the cost would be so immense that all the partying in the world just would not be worth it. But fuck me – those were the days!

Once we were done with The Woolpack, we took taxis to the gay village in Manchester which, on the face of it, might seem like a strange venue for a 12-strong gang of bodybuilding, hard-drinking thugs. However, there was method in the madness because the gay village definitely had its merits. First, it was a great place to party. And second, you're unlikely to get into any hassle in the gay village because, unlike the straight bars and clubs in town, the people in the gay village are there to party, not fight.

Our plan was to hit as many bars and clubs as we could, partying hard, drinking plenty and snorting obscene amounts of coke as we went – a pretty decent night out, and that would be the end of the story for most people. A bit of drinking, a few cheeky lines and a bit of a snog with a good looking bird if you're lucky. But I never was one for moderation. I never did know when to stop. I always had to push the boundaries and go one step further. More. More. Fucking more.

I don't remember exactly where we'd been, or where we were going, but on our way between bars we stumbled across a lad having a piss against one of the many bridges over the Manchester Ship Canal. I was in a typically giddy mood, as was always the case on our nights out. I was messing about and showing off, eager for the attention and adulation I'd come to expect from my crew, who seemed to love seeing me playing up, never knowing what would happen next.

As I got closer to the pissing lad I realised I knew him. It was John, a bloke I knew from Salford. My mind was racing with mischief and bravado, and out of seemingly nowhere an idea formed in my head. I came up behind him and grabbed his belt at the back of his trousers and, with my other hand, I grabbed the back of the collar of his shirt. Quick as a flash I lifted him off his feet to dangle, head first, over the bridge to stare into the filthy water below. I held him there for a few seconds, manically laughing as he screamed for mercy, much to the amusement of everyone around us. Eventually I pulled him back over the parapet, a look of abject fear fixed on his face. He looked to see who had done it, recognised me, and realised that there was absolutely nothing he could do about it.

And how we laughed. We laughed at the absurd piss take, and we laughed because we knew, no matter how much fear, and pain, and humiliation we had caused this person, we didn't give a fuck. And John laughed too, eventually, because he had no choice. He knew who we were and what we were capable of, and he knew that we could do whatever the fuck we wanted, because nobody wanted to get involved in a fight with a loony like me.

Then, out of the corner of my eye, I spotted a guy walking towards me. I was still laughing and arsing around with the lads, with the guy striding towards me with a cig hanging out of his mouth. He was a big fella too and, although I was still laughing, I'd already sized him up and was on full alert ready for a confrontation. "Yeah, funny mate. Try something like that with me I'll fucking hammer you!"

I didn't hesitate. I didn't talk back. I simply grabbed him by the throat and pushed him backwards, before tipping him over the bridge. This time I held him there for a second, looking at the fear plastered all over his face. And then I let go.

Believe it or not, the night's mayhem was not yet finished. The night had already been extreme by anyone's standards, but I continued to chase the thrills still higher. Always more. More. Fucking more.

Eager to impress, I ratcheted the absurdity up another notch. At the next bridge we came to I jumped over the parapet into the canal. In my drunken, cocaine-hazed state I can hardly remember what happened next, but I remember the cheering and the laughter, and I remember being dragged out of the water having somehow lost my shirt. In my eyes I was the craziest. I was the funniest. I was the wild man. And I wanted to carry on partying. I wanted more fun, more applause, more, more, fucking more.

Dripping wet and shirtless, me and the lads rocked up to a bar. The bouncers looked less than impressed. Quite understandably, we were lairy and looked like trouble. The doorman told us we weren't getting in. I probably don't need to go into detail but, needless to say, one thing led to another and I ended up in a fight, taking on the bouncer and his friend one after the other. I knocked one of them out, and the other backed down as he realised he was out of his league. Once it was over we continued our night of partying and mayhem in a different bar, me still shirtless and dripping wet. Lord knows how we gained entry, and God only knows how the evening ended, but likely at a party somewhere, where I would, as always, be the last man standing. That's how my evenings on the lash always came to a close.

At this point it might be difficult for you to understand how these events have anything to do with addiction. It might simply seem like the work of an irresponsible bully. And to a large degree, that would be true. But I assure you, it's all connected to addiction.

As you can tell, my addiction has always gone hand-in-hand with low self-esteem. From an early age I knew I was a piece of shit – the area we lived in, the broken home, the poverty we lived in compared with the swish, glossy lives we saw depicted on television and in the magazines. I couldn't compete and I couldn't compare. A lad like me from the streets I grew up in would never win if they played the game normal people played. I had to find another way to earn people's respect. So I became Shinny, the hard man, the player, the dealer, the clown, the addict.

Drinking and drugs smoothed out the despair. They made me feel happy and gave me the self-confidence I lacked when I was sober. No wonder I loved them so much. And the violence? That was my defence against people who disrespected me. Problem is, my low self-worth made me feel as if everyone was disrespecting me. Every minor slight, every bump on the dancefloor, every look in the wrong direction or word out of place – I took it as a sign of disrespect and answered it with violence. Drink, drugs, violence, narcissism, bullying and sex. They were all part of my addiction, and all fuelled by a self-loathing that festered deep in my stomach, making me feel like a piece of shit until the substances fooled me enough to think I was a messiah. That's what addiction does. The guy on the bridge, the doormen, the women I fucked that night and the obscene amounts of drink and drugs were all there to do one thing. They stopped me feeling like a piece of shit.

If only there was another way.

Puzzle piece 12

By 18 James had become addicted to steroids and cocaine, by this point the cocaine abuse had already taken full effect on his brain. Dopamine is the drug found in cocaine and it is also naturally produced in the brain. The large quantities endured were just about enough to surge his satisfaction and pleasure into oblivion for a short while. James' drug addiction and violent temper went hand in hand, with anger often a symptom of the drugs attacking the brain.

By now the increased paranoia, irrational thoughts, mood swings, and irritability had well and truly turned him into the well-known self-absorbed tyrant he had become. James' low self-esteem enticed him into drugs more and more due to the lack of faith in his own abilities. He was trapped in the life he had created in order to keep up the appearance of what seemed to be a young successful boy that had it all. In reality, he was lonely, angry and used his addiction to relieve how he felt inside. Now we meet the final stage; the superego… that we now know as Shinny.

PART 2.

WHAT'S YOUR SUPERPOWER?

CHAPTER 13.

WHEELS IN MOTION

If it weren't for Lee Butler, I wouldn't be who I am today. In fact, I believe there's a distinct likelihood that I wouldn't even be here at all. He probably doesn't realise it, but Lee Butler set the wheels in motion which, eventually, saved my life.

I'd known Lee for a few years because we knew some of the same people and he'd seen me play rugby at school. I bumped into him at the hospital when I was being treated for a broken hand I'd sustained while fighting. I'd told him to drop in anytime he was in the area. A few weeks later, to my surprise, he did just that. He rolled up in his grandad's old white Volvo and parked outside my mam's house. Turns out, he didn't have a licence either!

Once inside we started chatting about what each of us were up to, eventually getting into the subject of rugby. Lee played for Eccles Amateurs and was good friends with Adrian Morley who played for Leeds Rhinos and, later, for Great Britain. I was quite a big lad at the time, being well into my bodybuilding, but somehow I'd retained the speed I'd displayed when Lee saw me play at school. One thing led to another and I was eventually persuaded to come for a trial at Eccles.

It was a few weeks later that I made it to my first training session.

I turned up in flat-soled trainers and, even though it was pissing it down and I was slipping all over the place, I still outran most of the other players. Despite having little idea about the rules and strategies of rugby, I was strong, fast and aggressive – exactly what you need to be a good player. While the coaches had their reservations about letting me play, because I was still well known for my hard-partying drink and drugs lifestyle, the head coach decided to give me a chance.

Turns out, I was pretty good. I was so fast and aggressive that they couldn't ignore me and, within a few weeks, I'd earned a place in the team, taking over from players who had been at the club for years. Soon I was scoring tries, making a name for myself and frequently getting mentioned in the sports pages of the local paper. I carved a reputation as a rising star and, to me, it felt like I was becoming a celebrity.

Despite being well into my fitness, I was still partial to the occasional blow-out, and I was still selling drugs for a living. Although I was drinking less alcohol, I was still using drugs and, occasionally, to the extreme. You'll probably already know that drinking is a big part of rugby culture and so the compulsion to drink became very strong during my time in the game. I'm embarrassed to say that I also introduced drugs to the club, and I'll not be surprised if I'm responsible for instigating several drug habits among the club's former players. I remember taking coke up to away matches so that we could snort it on the coach on the way back home.

If I'm honest, the rugby itself didn't really appeal to me much, and I have no interest at all in rugby today. Being good at rugby was simply a platform for me to gain some respect and kudos – something which every addict needs. Addiction homes in on pursuits such as this as it ticks so many boxes. It gives us something to focus on intensely, something to completely dedicate ourselves to, and it gives us the recognition and respect we crave so much. So, the more attention I got, the harder I trained. It wasn't long before other clubs started to take interest in me.

Adrian Morley went to a school near to mine and we kinda knew each other in passing. I'd watched his rise to become one of the stars in the world of rugby, and I could only dream about achieving the kind of accolades and fame that Adrian had achieved. So, when I bumped into him at a local bar and learned that there was a chance I might play alongside him at Leeds Rhinos, I threw myself into the challenge – because that's what addicts do.

At the time I was getting something of a reputation, beyond that of just being a drug dealer and a gangster. In the rugby world I was known for my speed on the field and could run 100m on grass with my boots on in 10.5 seconds. I also held the record in the Conference League for scoring five tries in one game, so it was no surprise when Adrian Morley put my name forward to the Leeds head coach as an up-and-coming player. When I learned that there was a chance for me at Leeds Rhinos, I knew exactly what I had to do. All I could think about was how much extra training I needed to do, how much faster I could be, and how many steroids I'd need to take to make it happen.

I got invited for a trial at Leeds and played a few games for their reserve team, but I gradually realised that I was a very small fish in a very large pond. Instead of being the star of the show like I was at Eccles, I was just an average player among some extremely talented people. The fame and adulation I craved vanished, and I lost the confident buzz I got from being around people who liked and admired me. It was like someone had taken away my superpower, and my ego didn't like it one bit. Soon I was hammering the coke again, slacking on my training and losing all interest in what could have been one of the best opportunities of my life.

While I did play a few games for Salford, my rugby days were all but over, and addiction was entirely to blame. The addict's compulsive drive nosedived when the returns were not what my ego needed and expected. And anything which doesn't fuel the ego is of no use to the addict.

Before rugby was out of the picture I was already onto new things, looking for the next ego-lifting thrill. And what better, more appropriate thrill for an addict than the world of rock and roll.

Puzzle piece 13

James experienced many psychological stressors in early adulthood, both environmentally and emotionally. Common stressors for him were his absent father, no self-love, lack of self-respect, and the need to be bigger and better. The emotional signs of chronic stress have become predominant in the past few chapters, which include changes in his behaviour, as well as frustration, loss of emotional control, and self-medication. We possibly begin to see signs of ADHD, a disorder that has a worldwide prevalence in children and is four times more common in boys.

His hyperactivity and impulsivity caused difficulties in peer relationships meaning his social preference was low, he was less well-liked, and more than often rejected in social scenes. The respect and attention James craved was almost impossible to achieve as the character he projected was a narcissist and in turn, people were fearful of his violent tendencies and avoided him at all costs.

CHAPTER 14.

DURTY NELLY'S

Durty Nelly's was a well-known Irish pub and music venue in Bolton which was popular in the 1990s and early 2000s, and a regular hang-out for the lads from Eccles Rugby Club. I'd often been asked to come along for a night out, but had put it off for weeks for one reason or another. I was eventually convinced by fellow Eccles player, John McFadden, who had a regular slot at Nelly's playing guitar and singing. He was good too.

The first time I saw him on stage it nearly blew my mind. I remember getting a buzz of excitement, watching him on stage receiving all that adulation and applause. I felt an almost electric tingle as I imagined myself on stage, and I knew right there and then, that I wanted some of that too. The prospect of becoming a famous musician was all I could think about for days after seeing John play, and I spent hours working out what I had to do to make the dream come true. The following week I bought my first guitar, a Yamaha acoustic.

My biological father, Pete, had been pretty handy with a guitar and had been a big Bob Dylan fan (he'd also been a rugby player too, and I often wonder if that added to my compulsion to do those two pursuits as I did). Despite growing up in Manchester during the height of the UK's rave, dance and Madchester scenes, my musical tastes were always a bit different. I was listening to Pink Floyd and The Doors, when everyone else was listening to Oasis, The Stone Roses or The Happy Mondays. You have to remember, when I was growing up I was taking lots of LSD and imagining myself as Jim Morrison.

For the next couple of weeks I practiced ceaselessly during my every spare minute. I quit going to the gym and literally played until my fingers bled. I had little choice, in truth. I'd booked a spot to perform at Durty Nelly's in 14 days' time. Nobody knew what to expect from me after just two weeks of practice, but everyone I knew turned up to find out. I played Dylan's Tambourine Man and Knocking on Heaven's Door and, despite the fact that I was absolutely shitting myself the whole time, I went down a storm. Everyone was shocked, and the applause was deafening. And that was when I knew I wanted to be a musician. That kind of euphoria is something an addict simply can't resist.

Puzzle piece 14

It is possible that James could be suffering from what you could call the 'father wound'. This is the psychological, relational and physical dysfunction that happens with an individual whose father is emotionally or physically absent. For the most part, the 'father wound' separates into two parts, distance and anger or insecurity and clinginess. Coincidentally James was both; his life was filled with insecurity and misunderstandings which are created from unhealed issues.

James mirroring his father's activities could suggest an emotional attachment to his father. We also wonder why James wanted to indirectly connect to his father through rugby and music. In reality, we tend to notice the extraordinary voids in our life and in part can be a coping mechanism for dealing with loss.

CHAPTER 15.

OBSESSION OF THE MIND

By now, it should be as apparent to you as it is to me, that addicts tend to do things to the extreme. A big night out for most people isn't enough for an addict. We want more. Great sex and lots of love from one person isn't enough. We want more. Same goes for food, drink, exercise, happiness, rewards, respect, success – whatever it is that brings us pleasure or takes away pain, we want more of it. And therein, as far as I am concerned, lies the key to every addict's recovery.

Although I didn't realise it at the time, I'd already started to use my addiction as a superpower. It began with my efforts to cure my lisp, spending hours upon hours practising speaking properly. I knew that if I could lose the speech impediment, I'd eradicate much of the reason why people picked on me.

Then came bodybuilding. I threw myself into bodybuilding heart and soul, knowing that big, powerful men didn't have to worry about people picking on them. So, if everyone else trained three times a week, I trained five. If everyone else took steroids, I took more. The same happened with rugby, and then with music. Using the same compulsive tendencies and excesses that often push addicts towards destructive behaviour, we can, instead, choose to focus on constructive pursuits. That same compulsion and desire for more can create the kind of dedication that produces world-class athletes, superstar entertainers and the kind of academic and scientific minds that can change the world.

Think about it. You can't expect exceptional performance from a normal, average person. Normal people are, by definition, average, to some degree or another – and there's nothing wrong with that at all. The world needs stable, reliable people who don't create drama to keep the wheels of life turning smoothly. But, if it's extreme performance you need, you're going to need someone who can do things differently. You're going to need someone so bloody minded and dedicated that they won't falter at the first sign of difficulty. And there's nobody more committed and bloody minded than an addict.

I'm not saying that you need to have addictive tendencies in order to excel, but it's easy to see how people with addictive tendencies can become successful in their chosen field. How many actors can you name that are participating in the AA's 12-step program? How many celebrities have you seen go through rehab? How many sportspeople do you hear about going off the rails into addictive behaviours when their careers end? The numbers are staggeringly high, and this is no coincidence.

The reasons why these people choose these specific career paths is also obvious when you think about it in terms of what an addict needs. Of course, everyone needs love and a sense of personal achievement, but addicts need these things like they need food, air and water – they'd die without them, and many indeed do. That's why so many musicians, actors, politicians and sports people have problems with addiction. They were probably already addicts, but simply used their compulsion as a superpower to become supremely successful. These people typically become over-performing extreme-ists.

While I'm sure some addicts do become insurance salesmen or computer programmers, the needs of the addict will be with them too. How they deal with these needs and how much their addiction affects their life is not something we have the space to cover in this book. What I'm saying is, for myself, and for many addicts, it's death or glory. And for some addicts, it's both of those.

Much of my motivation for writing this book is an attempt to rebrand addiction and offer a different perspective on what this behaviour is. I'd like to break the stigma. There's no getting away from the fact that people with compulsive and obsessive personalities can form addictions to behaviours which will often ruin their lives. However, there is also another way. Many people with the same compulsive tendencies channel their obsession into more positive, constructive pursuits. Some become great actors, sportspeople or businesspeople, while others are great parents, Silicon Valley entrepreneurs or just plain good at whatever job they chose to do. The passion and dedication these people bring into the world is an undeniable force for good, so I feel it is enormously unfair to classify 'addictive' behaviours as universally bad. Addicts are simply unfortunate enough to have not (yet) channelled their compulsive behaviour into doing something worthwhile. They have yet to find their inner-superhero.

So, why is it that many people with such compulsive tendencies end up as addicts, while so few manage to channel their energy into something more positive? I guess I should begin this explanation by first stating the obvious – I'm no doctor. I'm not a scientist. I know nothing about psychology apart from what I've taught myself as part of my desire to manipulate people to do what I want them to do. Anyone who knows me will tell you I'm not very academic. However, I only need to have eyes in my head to see how compulsion affects people. I've met thousands of people and heard thousands of stories about how their compulsive behaviour has affected them. And I've lived it myself, so I think I have some insight into the situation, albeit unscientifically documented or tested.

What I do know is that many addicts start to go off the rails when they are children. Gabor Mate said that every addict has experienced childhood trauma, but not every child that has experienced trauma becomes an addict. Surely this is evidence that the addict was within us anyway and simply needed a catalyst to come out.

I believe the nightmare begins when we are learning who we are as people, when we are finding our way in the world, when we are working out what's right and wrong, what's good for us long term and what's going to cause us trouble in the long run. It begins when our brains are not fully formed enough for us to make good decisions. It starts because we don't have enough life experience to understand how the world works. It comes at a time when we are habitually reckless and can't yet see far enough into the future to comprehend that our bad behaviours of today will become life-destroying habits of the future.

And all of this is happening at a time when all kids are desperate for acceptance. It comes when most kids, even the popular ones, are vulnerable. Kids that age have no idea who they are, what their worth is or how they are supposed to behave. Many have low self-esteem and want nothing more than to feel like they belong. They want to be accepted and liked by their peers. They're desperate for acceptance and esteem, and they'll do anything to maximise their happiness and minimise their feelings of low self-worth. It's no wonder those kids who have a tendency for compulsive behaviour find ways to dedicate themselves to activities which limit their pain. That's why many turn to drink, drugs, violence, sex, food or any other pursuit which does the same job. If only we could help channel these kids into using their superpowers for something more rewarding.

I often think about what could have happened if someone had helped me in this way when I was young. I wonder what horrors I might have avoided, and I think about the levels of achievement I might have enjoyed, if only someone had told me that my compulsion could be used as a superpower. If only someone had shown me a path to happiness and explained how my superpower could be used to make my dreams come true. I can only hope that a kid like me will read this book and gain some benefit from it. God, please let that happen. I can't think of anything in the world I'd like more.

Puzzle piece 15

James is what you call a high-self monitor; they actively present an image to others that fit their audience. They monitor their presentation and how others are reacting and adjust it to try and achieve acceptance. High self-monitors are described as social chameleons and often may show behaviours that do not really reflect what they truly think. They are also more socially skilled but seem to have less committed social relationships.

A study found that being mistreated during childhood caused frequent and extremely high levels of stress that impeded normal brain development; triggering stress responses. These responses are likely to make victims of childhood traumatic experiences vulnerable to substance abuse disorders. The study also found that while counselling can help, around 5-10% get worse and 35-40% experience no benefit.

CHAPTER 16.

SEX, DRUGS AND ROCK AND ROLL

My rock and roll career took off at about the same time my rugby career fizzled out. I'd been disinterested and slack about rugby from the moment I realised I wasn't the rugby superstar I wanted to be at Leeds Rhinos and, while I played a handful of games for Lancashire and for England Under 21s, the drug-dealing and my new-found rock- star passion soon took over altogether. From there, things moved really fast. From my nervous first gig at Durty Nelly's in Bolton, it was less than four years before I was supporting New Order. That's what the dedication of an addict can achieve.

After a few weeks of banging out cover songs on my new guitar I was writing my own tunes, the first being a song about Holly called Sunny Sundays. Soon, I'd recruited several other musicians to form a band, which we called Hanky Park after the area in Salford near where I'd grown up. Strangely, the first line-up included a singer – an arrangement which, in retrospect, was doomed to fail. He was good, but there was no way the ego-maniac inside me would allow someone else to be the front-man in the limelight. I wanted the adoration all for myself. Within a few months we were gigging constantly, hitting the Manchester music circuit hard. We released our first demo CD, called Took You For Granted, in 2003.

We stood out from the other bands doing the rounds at that time in several ways. I was a notorious bad-boy with a reputation that preceded me. Most bands would get only £1 of the £5 ticket price. Me being me, I 'negotiated' a 50/50 deal. Plus, I was well known enough to be pulling in decent crowds night-after-night. With big door receipts and us getting 50%, we were making a bit of money.

By now we had crossed the radar of several big-name players in the Manchester music scene, not least Peter Hook from Joy Division and New Order. He'd heard about us and our big following of punters and invited us to support his side-project band, Monaco. Seeing our name on posters in Manchester was a massive buzz and it felt like we'd hit the big time.

Over time, Hooky and I became good friends, as did Tony Wilson, the owner of the infamous Hacienda club, and between them, they managed to spread word of our crazy band far and wide and deep into the music scene. Manchester was buzzing with Hanky Park.

Eventually, Hooky called me up and asked us to support New Order at short notice. I was on a cruise-ship holiday at the time, but I flew home from Greece to do the show, before flying back out to re-join the boat. Playing in front of thousands of people was fucking heaven for me. We absolutely rocked that place and the applause and cheers filled me with everything I'd ever needed and wanted.

From there, things blew up for us big time. We went on to support New Order at shows all over the UK. We were also headlining our own shows, making the papers and tipped to be the next big thing. In just four years I went from zero musical ability to the very edge of making it in the big-time but, of course, my inability to manage my demons fucked it all up.

The rock and roll scene is known for its excess. Rock stars have been overdosing and drinking themselves into early graves since forever, so it should be no surprise to anyone that I was easily seduced into the crazy lifestyle. And then, there were the adoring female fans – the deadly trio of sex, drugs and rock and roll. It was addictive behaviour at its best, and its worst at the same time. Such focus and drive is a powerful tool when it's properly harnessed, but it will fuck you up big time if you use it badly. And I fucking went for it, big time!

Puzzle piece 16

Addiction can be related to mental health problems, however, the start of addiction can stem from trying to cope with feelings you are unable to deal with. From what we hear about James he becomes self-obsessed; the more he gets the more he wants, and for a person with an addictive personality, roaring overwhelming crowds of people fed him with the praise he desired.

However, the image that some people see of this socially outcast musician was an inaccurate version of the individual he had become, who was addicted to reassurance, gratification and drugs. James may have also been showing signs of OCD (obsessive-compulsive disorder), as one time was never enough and in turn, he harmed relationships, promoted avoidance and validated his obsession.

CHAPTER 17.

THE BOXER

Jamie Moore was the British Light Middleweight boxing champion. I knew of him because of his boxing fame, and he knew of me because of my gangster, drugs, rugby and rock and roll infamy. When we met we hit it off immediately and became best of friends for years. Jamie even used one of my songs, Crazy Guy, for his walk-out music on fight nights.

At the time I was a 15 stone (95kg) bodybuilder and rugby player, well-built and athletic. Plus, I knew how to fight, so the move to boxing was as natural as wiping my arse. The gym was run by legendary former boxer Steve 'The Viking' Foster, and as soon as I put on the gloves and started banging away at the bag Steve said he knew I had talent.

I don't know if it was a test to see if I had what it took to make it in boxing, but Steve told me I needed to slim down from 15 stone to light-middleweight. For most people it's not easy to cut weight, especially to that extent, but for me and my obsessive abilities, it was a piece of piss. I dieted like my life depended on it, and I trained twice a day before my first amateur fight which I won by TKO (technical knockout). Though, to be honest, I was glad the fighter didn't come out for the third round because, in typical Shinny fashion, I'd gone all out and given it everything I had and was completely fucked.

After just one amateur fight I decided I wanted to turn professional, my motivation being 'Fuck the trophies, I want the money'. With only one amateur fight behind me, in order to get my pro licence I had to spar in front of the boxing board to convince them of my ability. This was no problem for me because I'd already been sparring with Jamie Moore and several other pros at the gym, so I'd picked up skills pretty quickly and I completely looked the part.

Before I knew it I had my first pro fight booked at Salford Rugby Club in front of a crowd of around 2000 punters, pretty much all of whom were there to see me. My notoriety meant I was an immediate crowd puller, so the fight commanded a decent purse. Again, I won, knocking my opponent out in the 5th round. The disease loved it – the extreme dedication to diet and training, the tough-guy bravado, the adulation and hero worship, the crowds, the cheering, the women, the money and the all-out mayhem of it all. This was my yard, my people, my stage, and I fucking loved it. It was a passion that I could be extreme with and violence that was acceptable.

Yet, despite the distraction and accolades of boxing, I was still addicted to drugs. I was still training hard and staying off the gear when I was in the preparation stages of a fight, but outside those times I was burning the candle at both ends and hitting the drugs hard. After every period of clean living and hard training, I'd come back to the drink and drugs harder than before.

Two weeks before my fourth fight I had been high on cocaine for two days solid. I knew I had a fight coming up, but my ego had caused me to believe I was indestructible. I honestly thought a two-day coke binge wouldn't affect my performance. Needless to say, I was very fucking wrong.

I don't want to take anything away from my opponent, Paul Lomax, because he was a good fighter who might have beaten me regardless. However, there's no question that my drink and drug fuelled body was not prepared for the beating I received in that fight. In short, I got fucking hammered and ended up being stretchered out of the ring, unable to stand up or speak. I spent a day in hospital in such a bad way that I truly believed I would never be able to speak or walk properly again.

I heard later that the referee was suspended for letting the fight carry on as long as it did. I'd been so badly beaten up that I was clearly not in a position to defend myself, but the ref had let me fight on. Once again, my extreme-ist tendencies and my inability to stay off the drugs had fucked my life up good and proper.

Although boxing had offered some kind of salvation, I wasn't yet ready to give up the drugs. The gaps in between the fights gave my naïve and vulnerable ego too much opportunity to revert back to the lifestyle that I knew and loved. I didn't have the awareness to do anything different. I hadn't done the work I needed to do to understand addiction and extreme-ism, I didn't know that I was constantly chasing something. While I knew how to stop for a while, I just couldn't stay stopped.

It would take a lot more sorrow and heartache, and a lot more thinking about myself and my illness, before I could quit being an addict and turn my extreme-ism for the good.

PUZZLE PIECE 17

The word addiction is derived from a Latin term for 'enslaved by' or 'bound to'. A study has found that 40-60% of susceptibility to addiction is hereditary, however environmental factors play a big role when it comes to reinforcing the habit.

When James would engage in something satisfactory the release of dopamine to the brain would take full effect. This would mean that the short-term pleasure he was feeling would present itself to James as if it was something that actually made him happy; in reality, it was the opposite. When the 'buzz' from boxing would wear off he would feel the need for the fix of another dopamine rush... turning right back to cocaine.

CHAPTER 18.

Welcome to the World, Son

Becky was the sister of a mate of mine, and everyone was worried when it became obvious that I had my eye on her. Still, what SHINNy wants, SHINNy gets, and it wasn't long before Becky and I were together.

I was not only taking and selling copious amounts of coke, by this time I'd also developed a liking for crack. It started with just the occasional visit to a crack den, but I already knew that I loved it more than any other drug I'd ever taken. The first time had hit me like a ton of bricks — it was like coke, but a hundred times better. We extreme-ists always love stuff that gives you more.

As you can imagine, it didn't take long for my relationship with Becky to reach breaking point. Just two years after we'd got together, we'd split up and Becky went on holiday to Spain with some friends to get her head together. Little did I know at the time that she was pregnant and had gone away with her friends to contemplate her options. When she came back to the UK she got in touch and told me she was pregnant and that I was going to be a dad.

I'd assumed that she and I would get back together, but Becky took some persuading. However, we eventually sorted our shit out, got a place to live together and made it ready for our child. Donovan was born on the 27th of January 2004. Becky was 20 and I was 27, and I was dead serious that I was going to clean up my act. I decided this was the kick up the arse I needed and that I would get sober, stop selling gear and earn a living legally. And, for a while, I did just that.

Becky and I built ourselves a home, I stopped dealing and quit drinking and taking drugs. I even set up a legitimate business with Becky's brother, leaning on his experience in the double-glazing trade. To the untrained eye, everything looked peachy. But underneath the addiction was still raging inside me. Only this time, my problem was much worse. This time, it was crack.

It didn't take long for the mask to slip. On the day Donovan was born Becky encouraged me to 'go wet the baby's head', probably expecting that her consent to have a few beers would stop me from going too crazy. Of course, me being me, I went on a crack bender, arriving home fucked up, pinned out of my face, to be greeted by Becky, her mum and my new-born son. In retrospect, it must have been mortifying.

Soon it was all falling apart around me. The crack benders became more frequent and lasted for days at a time. Neither could I resist the ease at which I could make the occasional large-scale drug deal, bringing in big chunks of money. It's hard to turn your back on that kind of easy money. I was also dabbling in the occasional dodgy deal and fraud jobs when the opportunity arose, or when I needed cash for bills or drugs. Eventually my business partner and I couldn't work together, so I got rid of him and tried to go it alone, employing people with the skills I lacked. And, of course, there were the women. Becky knew what was going on, and she hated me for it.

After three years of mayhem, Becky had finally had enough. She called me up while I was driving and told me it was over. She was leaving me and taking my child with her. I pulled over and broke my heart. I'd lost Becky and I'd lost my son. I'd fucked it all up proving that, once again, what a no-good no-hope loser I was.

It was a perfect excuse to fuck more women and take more crack. And I did that to the fucking extreme, like any good addict would, under the circumstances. Adversities are like a rumbling stomach to an addict. It needs to be fed.

Puzzle piece 18

This short-lived high dragged James back every time, with the slightest inconvenience diving him straight back into addiction. The exceptional high is quickly followed by intense depression, edginess and a craving, adding to the increased emptiness he already felt. Coming down from that kind of drug causes severe depression, which becomes deeper and deeper after each use, so severe that a person will do anything to get the drug.

Stats show that UK homicide rates highlight that 31% of victims and suspects are under the influence of alcohol and drugs at the time of death. These physical, emotional and environmental risks would have left James more vulnerable than he already was.

PART 3.

AIMING FOR ROCK BOTTOM

CHAPTER 19.

CRACKING UP

I couldn't quit boxing after a loss. I eventually recovered after the battering I received in the last fight to Lomax and was booked on the undercard of a Joe Calzaghe fight at the Manchester MEN Arena. Although I was clean during training and worked hard for the win, I was still a slave to my addiction and went back to the booze, coke and crack as soon as the fight was over. I could put down the drink and drugs as long as I was feeding my addict with something equally as extreme and thrilling.

Despite all I'd been through with my addiction, I still wasn't ready to change. No amount of destroyed relationships, wasted opportunities, upset family members or even losing my own son was enough for me to see sense. These events provided excuses to take drugs. I knew my life was a mess, and I knew I had a serious problem with drink and drugs, but I just didn't have the right brain in my head to understand that change was necessary and how much work was needed to make even a start at quitting. Even if I'd had access to a mentor, someone who had been there and done it, even if they had sat me down and explained the situation to me in great detail, I simply wouldn't have listened. I was sure I knew best when that was clearly not the case.

After Becky left my drug abuse went into overdrive. I was shagging anything that moved and I was smoking more crack than ever. While my intake of drugs could be described as legendary, I was still gigging with Hanky Park and was booked to do a slot at Salford Rugby Club for rugby pro Malcolm Alker's testimonial.

As per usual, the gig and the after-party involved snorting copious amounts of coke and ecstasy. By the next day, after not going to bed the night before, I was in a bar with some friends and noticed my hands had started to swell. I was a bit concerned, but my mates laughed it off, saying they didn't know how big my hands were supposed to be. I eventually laughed it off too and carried on partying, but I was becoming increasingly aware that the swelling was now affecting my feet as well.

I eventually made my way home and, feeling fucking awful, went to bed with my hands, feet and face swollen and painful to the touch. Sometime in the early hours of the morning I called Jamie Moore and told him I was dying.

By the time Jamie arrived I could hardly move or speak. My hands and feet had swollen to the point where they were almost comical, as had my cock and my balls. My mouth was ablaze with ulcers and everything was red, inflamed and so painfully sore I can't describe it. Jamie told me later that he was convinced I was going to die in the back of his car as he sped me to the hospital.

I spent three weeks in Hope hospital. My whole body was covered in blisters, and my skin peeled off like a shedding snake. I was given opiates to control the pain, but they didn't touch it – probably due to the resistance I'd built up after so many years of drug abuse. And all the time I was in there, while I couldn't speak, wracked with pain and watching my family in tears, thinking I was going to die, all I could think was "This has to stop!" I knew that I had almost left my son without a father, and so I swore on my son's life that I would never drink or use drugs again.

What a load of utter bollocks that was.

Within three months of leaving hospital, after all my promises to my family and myself that I would stop, I was back drinking and using worse than ever. I'm not sure how it started, but as always, it was probably nothing major. It would usually be that I'd allow myself a shandy, or a lager with a lemonade top, but that's all the disease needs to take hold again. After a period of sobriety addicts convince themselves that they 'didn't have a problem after all' and congratulate themselves with the exact poison that had been destroying their lives.

For addicts, it's not the 20th drink that fucks you up, it's the first one. Alcoholics have no defence against alcohol and just one drink is all it needs to take hold and run riot through your life once more. As I've said repeatedly, we can't do anything in moderation. If I'm going to drink, I'm going to drink until it's all fucked up and everything around me is ruined. I just want more, more, fucking more. It wasn't as if I didn't know I was spiralling out of control. Everywhere I looked my life was a mess, but I just didn't have the knowledge or the ability to stop. I'd lost my son, fucked up relationships and almost died, but I was still a full-blown addict.

Puzzle piece 19

By now we notice a few things about James, he is upset if ignored, he believes he can always be bigger and better, his self-esteem is very fragile and most importantly, he always puts his own needs first. All of which could point to a certain illness called narcissistic personality disorder.

For most people, a near-death experience would be enough to scare the life out of you, for James this wasn't the case. In fact, it is possible that he could not cope with the overwhelming idea of abandoning his child just like his father did to him. Bringing these abandonment issues to life eventually led James right back to what made him feel comfortable and reassured; drugs.

CHAPTER 20.

SECOND CHANCE

It was my friend Lee who introduced me to crack – not that I blame him at all. Let's be honest here, I would have started doing crack one way or another. Lee and I had been mates for years, using and abusing drugs together, so we were pretty close as mates go. Then, in August 2009, Lee had a tragic accident, falling off a roof in Magaluf. He was off his head at the time and trying to get into his apartment by climbing onto the balcony. It didn't end well. Lee's head injury has left him with permanent and serious disabilities. It would be rather dark to say that Lee's accident did at least have one positive outcome, but that's how I met my daughter's mother, Ashley.

Lee was on holiday with Claire, his partner at the time, and Claire had a sister called Ashley. When I flew over to Magaluf to support Lee in the aftermath of the accident, Ashley flew out to support her sister. I knew the first moment I saw her that I had to have her and, despite the awful circumstances, my disease took hold and I set the wheels in motion to make it happen.

Ashley was typical of the type of woman I needed to be with, but she was also different in many ways. My own chaotic, destructive life needed to be balanced by women who had their shit together, and Ashley certainly fit the bill. She had spent 10 years in the Navy and had a great career at Hopwood Hall College helping to train naval recruits. The difference was that Ashley was quite unlike the fiery, volatile women I'd been with before. She was strong, successful and beautiful, and she was calm, professional and rational — and she was well out of my league.

Lucky for me, and unluckily for Ashley, I had a few tricks up my sleeve. Years of addiction had made me into a master manipulator and I was able to use my skills to convince her into a relationship with me. An addict's cunning is a superpower that can be used for both good and evil – and Lord help everyone if we use it for evil, because the consequences will always catch up with you in the end.

In the beginning we were awesome. We had a great time drinking and partying together, her moderation helping to keep my extremeist tendencies in check. Yeah, I was still drinking and using, but being with Ashley helped me to keep my shit together and the show on the road – at least for a while anyway. But when Ashley fell pregnant five months later, I reverted to type and was soon back to my old ways, and worse. Ashley being pregnant meant she was no longer up for partying and, without my moderator, it was back to the madness and mayhem for me.

I've talked enough about how fucked up I would get and how hard the addiction took hold each time I gave it an opportunity, so there's no need for me to go over it all again now, but I recall Ashley being eight-months pregnant and me frantically begging in writhing sobs of tears for her to drive me to a crack-house in Bolton because I needed a fix so badly. She drove me there and sat outside that crack house in the car for almost two hours waiting for me. You might ask why she would help me to get drugs when we both knew it was killing me, but you have to remember that a crack addict in need is a terrifying and desperate sight. Looking back it's mortifying to think about what I put that woman through, but at the time I was powerless and had no control over my compulsions and addictions.

Our daughter was born on the first of September 2010, and we called her Gracie Lee in honour of our friend who had the accident in Magaluf. It should have been a joyous time, but when the father of the baby is a full-blown crack-head, it was anything but. I was still going on benders and regularly fucking random women.

Although I wasn't dealing drugs at the time I was still making money from other illegal exploits which I can't go into here, while also trying to still run a business working in the building trade. By now I had realised that I couldn't be a drug dealer because there was no way I could resist getting high on my own supply. I'd already fallen foul of this plenty of times in the past when I'd been dealing and had, predictably, become my own best customer.

It can seem strange to those who don't know addicts to see someone like me, destroyed by drink and drugs on one hand, but then holding it together enough to have a business and use the gym too. I didn't look like a junkie dropout. I was just a fucking nightmare.

Holding it together is an illusion — a thin veneer. The only way I can explain it is like walking a tightrope, where you're always on the edge of falling into the abyss of being that stereotypical derelict junkie, but holding it together just enough to be a father (of sorts), run a business (kinda), appear like you're normal(ish) — just enough to get by. Everyone who knew me could see that it was an act, but I'd somehow convinced myself that my definition of normal was close enough. To everyone else I was a fucking no-mark addict, but I felt like I was playing the system and beating the odds.

Like all of the women I've ever had in my life, Ashley kept me from falling off the edge by filling in the gaps when I failed, and by mopping up the mess when I fucked it up completely. She paid the bills, she looked after the kids, she kept the house in order and, when she could, steered me away from the self-destructive mayhem that I would inevitably bring down upon my family. She was always there to clean up after me, until, one day, she wasn't.

I'd already been convinced by my disease that Ashley and baby Gracie Lee were holding me back. The addict-deranged half of my brain was telling me that they were an obstruction to my drinking and using, and the other, more sane part of my brain eventually gave up objecting and started to buy into the bullshit. I would start arguments and become frighteningly aggressive. I was convinced that she was cheating, even though I knew she wasn't, but my paranoid brain somehow managed to make me believe it. My disease wanted them out of the picture and, eventually, it won. During one of our many arguments Ashley told me she was leaving.

It was two weeks before I heard from Ashley again, when she called me up and told me that we needed to talk. We met up at the house and talked for hours, discussing what needed to happen for us to have a life together. Somehow, after all I'd put her through, Emma was willing to give me one last chance.

We kissed and made up, and while Ashley was in the bathroom I texted the other girl I'd been seeing and told her it was over, before putting my phone down on the table. When the reply to my text came through, Ashley read the message on the screen, before picking it up to show me what she'd seen. It read: "I'm going to miss what we had, SHINNy". Understandably, Ashley lost her shit and, finally, that was it. We were finished.

The severity of the situation descended on me immediately. Once again, I'd destroyed a relationship and lost another family. Once again, my world came crashing down around me as my chance at redemption and a normal family life was left in tatters by my behaviour. I'd failed again, and the extent of my failure destroyed my fragile ego, highlighting without any shadow of a doubt the kind of loser I was. I flew into a fit of rage before going outside to smash up Ashley's car, resorting to the one talent I knew I could always rely on.

In the years since Ashley and I have discussed how we got into the mess that we did. For me, it's obvious, and what happened was no surprise at all, but for a long time, Ashley couldn't understand how she let herself become involved with someone as fucked up and dangerous as I was. She blamed herself for the situation she found herself in. It took a lot of explaining and apologising after I got well before she could get her head around how we'd ended up in the situation we did.

It's important to add that I truly did love Ashley, as I had Becky and Holly. I hadn't set out to hurt them or make their lives a nightmare. Many times I'd been absolutely adamant and determined to quit drinking and using, but I couldn't. As hard as I tried to be a good partner, parent, friend, my alcohol and drug-fuelled ego caused me to destroy every good thing I'd ever had. I wish I could turn the clock back. I wish I knew then what I know now. I wish a lot of things had turned out differently. But there's no going back, and that's probably for the best. The best thing we can do, as addicts, is to make the future better somehow. We have to find ways to recover, make amends for our past and avoid making the same mistakes again.

Unfortunately, despite my desperate hope, and despite all I'd learned about addiction to date, I wasn't ready to change. I wasn't ready to recover. History would repeat itself again and again and again.

Puzzle piece 20

We can't always say addiction and behaviour form from the environments and situations one finds themselves in. James' genetic vulnerability contributed to the risk of developing an addiction. Everything he did his brain would register pleasure in the same way whether that be reassurance, sexual encounters or even a satisfying meal. Within the brain lies a reward centre, which has a particular area called the hippocampus where it lays down memories; embedded deep into the temporal lobe. This means it creates the memories of something satisfactory, such as drugs. At this point James is what you could call a high functioning addict, he was addicted to the substance but could still project an outward appearance of normality.

CHAPTER 21.

Don't call it a comeback

The only time I'd ever been able to properly stop drinking and using was when I was preparing for a fight. I'd done it before and, as far as I was concerned, I could do it again. For me it was not only easy to spend eight or nine weeks eating healthy, training hard and staying clean and dry, it was a fucking joy. Dedicating myself to something, working hard at it and thrashing myself in the gym until my eyes bled was an absolute pleasure. It made me feel strong, capable, in control and indestructible. Not only that, it enhanced the image I always wanted to project. It told people I was not somebody to be fucked with. Boxing was custom built for my needs.

But, with my life having fallen to pieces once again, I was desperate for a way to get back on top. While boxing was something I could throw myself into and excel at, my primary motivation this time around was survival because, in my mind, boxing offered my only chance of redemption.

I made an appointment to see Jamie Moore at the gym and begged him to arrange another fight and, to my utter amazement, he agreed. Again, there's something about an addict in need that can charm the birds from the trees. A date was set, an opponent was found and my training began in earnest.

True to my word I quit the substances and trained like a madman. Word got out that Shinny was back in training and a kind of buzz seemed to be occurring everywhere I went. The Manchester Evening News even picked up the story and published the article as being my salvation from addiction. For the next eight weeks I felt amazing. I was in my element and loving every minute of it. It was me, doing what I do best and right at the top of my game, As the fight date neared I felt I was more than ready. I'd been clean for eight weeks and got myself into phenomenal shape. I was a machine. I was back from the brink, bigger, faster, stronger and tougher than ever.

And then, at the eleventh hour, the boxing board revoked my licence.

Part of the administration checks before a fight involves a health report from your doctor, and mine had listed the anti-depressant medication I'd been prescribed for my mental health. I was fucking devastated. These drugs were by no means a performance-enhancing drug but the board took my licence away anyway. I was given no opportunity to challenge the decision and no time to put an appeal together. They closed it down and the fight was cancelled. That fight was to be my salvation, and they snatched it away from right in front of me.

Predictably, my life went into nosedive. The news destroyed my soul, leaving me feeling worthless yet again. Feeling worthless is the worst feeling an addict can have and the one stress most likely to lead to relapse. And boy, did I relapse! I'd found the bottom plenty of times before, but this time it was worse than ever.

It's often the case for addicts to relapse harder and deeper than they have done before, as if the last low point wasn't quite low enough. Coupled with the fact that they do not have the same resistance to the substance after a period of sobriety. For me it was as if I'd proved to myself that I was able to recover from the last low, no matter how close to the edge I'd come. So, having hit some pretty fucking low points before, I went out hard to achieve a new, lower level.

The crack benders became something that would happen every

weekend and, while I managed to hold down a job, the drinking and drugs were a daily ritual. I was regularly using women, hassling my mum for money to feed my drink and drug habits.

I'd spend days at a time in crack houses and we all now know what happened there! I was surrounded by a surprisingly diverse array of people, from seemingly successful folk with nice clothes and cars, families and jobs, to the worst scum of the earth on death's door with nowhere to go but down. Often these places would be empty walls with no furniture, stinking of piss and sweat and puke, and I felt entirely comfortable being there. By now, I had no pride left to lose and a gaping hole where my self worth was taken. Worth that was accumulated by success and a desire to be outwardly successful.

Puzzle piece 21

The intense craving created by a conditioned response in the brain could not be stopped for James. He went from liking, to wanting, to needing. The house James would go to could have supplied him with a small amount of relief, surrounded by people just like himself.

Hidden from society, this place was somewhere he could not be judged or feel the need to be bigger and better, in retrospect they were all the same, just at different stages and capability within addiction. You could say James was in the middle of this metaphorical stage, but in hindsight, he was far from the top and on the way to the bottom.

CHAPTER 22.

REACHING THE BOTTOM

It would be a bit misleading to say that any particular event represented me hitting rock bottom because, in reality, there were many, many rock bottoms. Any one of those occasions could, and probably should, have been severe enough to kick off some kind of recovery. But, for whatever reason and another, it took many rock bottom experiences to make it happen. I'd destroyed so many chances and damaged so many people during my time as an addict. Every one of the women I've mentioned in this book was more forgiving and supportive than could be expected of any person, but each time I reached rock bottom with them, I'd start the cycle all over again with a new partner, a new safety net, a new victim.

My recovery journey has helped me to understand that I am enormously co-dependant. I simply cannot cope on my own. I'm unstable, chaotic and destructive without a calming influence from someone who is strong-willed enough to counter my otherwise forcibly destructive tendencies. When I'm on my own I have only my thoughts to live with, and left to their own devices my thoughts would inevitably lead me to dark, dangerous and destructive places – such is the power of an unchecked addiction. I need the help of a strong-willed woman.

Holly, Becky, Ashley and, all of those since deserve the highest of praise for helping me when we were together, despite the appalling stuff I put them through. I was attracted to strong women because they were the only partners strong enough to stick with me through those dreadful times. They were with me because they had the resilience and determination to try to help me, and I loved them for that. I was attracted to their power and used it to my advantage. And in return, I broke their hearts and destroyed their lives. I loved them dearly, and I desperately wanted our relationships to work, but the disease inside me would inevitably destroy us. Time after time after time.

Kate Brown was known to me as Kat from the gym. I'd known her for years and we frequently flirted but hadn't got together until Ashley and I split up. She knew me of old and was aware of my wild reputation, but I can't imagine she had any idea how bad I really was.

Because who in their right mind would get together with someone as damaged and dangerous as I was.

Naively, Kate or Kat, as I'd call her, moved into my house with her two kids, and we played happy families for a few months before the extent of my addiction became clear. I'd manipulated another woman into my life, and the mayhem would soon be upon us, but in the meantime, I was still causing suffering for the mothers of my children.

Looking back at the events of that time there were many occasions which could be identified as a turning point for my journey from addiction to recovery, but if I look at it closely, the beginning of the end of my addiction can be traced to the morning of Donovan's school sports day. I'd been out all night on a crack and cocaine bender and, by the morning of the event, I hadn't yet sobered up from the drugs and the drink I'd thrown down my neck. As the morning wore on I got worse, not better, and knew that I'd need a few drinks down me to stop the shaking if I was going to make it. I needed a 'pick-me-up', so I skulled a few cans. Even though I was fucked up and looked like shit, I knew I had to get to the sports day. I couldn't let my kids down like our dad had done to us. I had to make it there, no matter what, so off I went.

I looked and smelled awful, my face ashen and drawn with the typical crack-head horror story. It was midday by the time I'd got enough beer inside me to contemplate leaving the house and I turned up at Donovan's school looking like a fucking junkie. Everyone there saw me for what I was, but I honestly thought I was doing OK, such was my delusion that I could appear normal.

I tried my best, but I was quite obviously wasted, slurring, falling over and cracking inappropriate jokes with Becky and her mum, who both did their best to shield Donovan from seeing his dad in such a state. Becky asked me if I'd been drinking, to which I replied: "Yeah, so what?" Midday was an acceptable time to be drinking, in my messed-up world. I didn't realise it at the time, but Becky had reached the limits of her tolerance and was making a plan to put a stop to it.

It was a few weeks later that I received a call from a friend of mine, Cappo, who told me that he'd seen Becky and Ashley together in a local café. Although the mothers of my children knew each other, they weren't friends and would have had no reason to be socialising – unless, of course, they were plotting against me. Which, to their credit, they absolutely were.

A couple of weeks later I took calls from both Becky and Ashley in turn, telling me that they would not let me see my children again unless I sorted myself out. The risks to the children's physical and psychological wellbeing were too great. And they were absolutely right.

At first, I was ablaze with anger but gradually I processed the situation I faced and realised that I'd become the very thing I despised. I'd come to terms with the fact that I'd destroyed the relationships I'd had with these women and that I had ruined the family life I could have enjoyed. I knew that I'd fucked that up.

But, despite all that, I had consoled myself with the knowledge that I was still the father of my children. My children were the one thing I had in my life that was worth living for, and being a good father was my last shred of dignity. And now, this had been taken away from me. I was literally nothing.

MAKING OF AN ADDICT

I already knew I was an addict. I already knew I was a worthless, weak and destructive loser, and the only thing that had stopped me committing suicide before now was the fact that I was a father to two wonderful children. I longed to be a good father to my children and give them the kind of relationship I'd craved when I was a kid. My relationship with my biological father, Pete, had been destructive enough for me to not wish that kind of suffering on anyone. And when he left our lives, I was so hurt that I knew I needed to be a different kind of dad — yet here I was doing the same thing to my own kids.

I knew that if I wasn't a father I may as well be dead.

Puzzle piece 22

If we put infidelity to one side, James was in fact still maintaining multiple relationships. In reality, he was in an intimate relationship with the women passing through his life while keeping his emotional relationship with drugs. Individuals who do not take drugs are seen as strong and in a healthy relationship with themselves.

The image of James we have in our mind right now emphasises that he does not understand love or how to love himself as much as he should. This is problematic for James when it comes to developing a strong relationship foundation. Being fatherless often results in a child blaming themselves for their absent parent, this no doubt had a negative impact on his self-esteem, leading him to continuously search for something to fill that void. Would James have still become an addict if his father were present?

CHAPTER 23.

SURRENDER

They say that only when you have lost everything can you begin to rebuild your life. I'd not yet reached the bottom of my addiction, but losing my children gave me all the motivation I needed to sink deeper down. I wanted to get better, but I knew I didn't have what it took. I had tried so many times and failed. People had tried to help me, and I'd destroyed them. And now, my drinking and drug abuse were worse than ever, so there was little hope that I could make it out of this alive.

And, without Kat, I am certain that death would have taken me. She was there at my lowest point and helped me through the absolute worst of my addiction. I'd reached the point where I was drinking 24/7. If my eyes were open, I was drinking. I was taking more drugs more often than ever before, and suffering from the worst withdrawal symptoms imaginable.

I didn't have normal hangovers, I had nervous fucking breakdowns. Each night I'd drink myself into oblivion and hit the crack-pipe until I simply couldn't hit it anymore. And, the next day, I'd wake up a shivering, crying, fucked up mess. It's difficult to describe the scene, but believe me, it's the worst kind of hell. Crack addicts in need are described as 'rattling'. A twitching, tense knot churns in your stomach while you dry-retch a vomit that simply won't come up. I can't think of how it feels without an adrenaline-infused terror filling my mind with both dread and yearning at the same time.

The need for alcohol is similarly twisted. I'd be physically tensed up in a ball, fists clenched, shouting, "GET ME A DRINK!" through my tightly gritted teeth, hallucinating as I lay there drenched in sweat. Whether it's crack or alcohol, when withdrawal has got you, your whole body can't do anything except beg for the mercy only a drink or a pipe will bring. Despite the physical, chemical and biological effects of these drugs, I'm convinced that the majority of the suffering was psychological, because as soon as I saw someone arrive with a bag full of beer, or when the dealer turned up with my fix, my body would relax and a feeling of elation and calm would wash over me before I'd even got the drug inside me. Addiction is a mental disease for sure.

And the triggers for recovering alcoholics are immense. Even talking about it now makes me retch, just like I did when suffering withdrawal, and simply the thought of what it was like makes me frightened and wary. I'm sure just talking about it and reliving the experience in my head would mean I'd be likely to find myself in a crack-house before the day is through - if it wasn't for the strength I found through my recovery to resist the urges. This disease will suck you back in if there's any sign of weakness to be found.

It had taken four years of mayhem to finally reach where I was at that point, and the last seven or eight months while I was with Kat were the absolute worst of it. I was angry and depressed about losing my children. I'd gone from hero to zero in the eyes of my son and I was suicidal, with my only relief being more drink and drugs. And it was Kat who was there through it all. She witnessed it all – drink, breakdown, drink, repeat for month-upon-months on end. Kat was the backbone of my world; the most solid human being I could hope to have beside me. She was much more than I deserved, but she was on my side.

I knew I had a serious, life-threatening problem, but I had no idea what to do about it. My only route to recovery that had worked to any degree before was boxing, and that option had been taken away from me. I was at a loss, but Kat somehow convinced me to get in touch with the local drugs and alcohol services.

I'd been to an Alcoholics Anonymous meeting before, back in 2012 and had been distinctly unimpressed. I'd met a guy there who had been sober for eight years and thought to myself, "Well, why the fuck are you still coming to these fucking stupid meetings then?" And when I heard them mention God, I decided AA was a fucking joke. As you can imagine, I was reluctant to get back into any formal treatment program, because who wants to be around all those losers who I had nothing in common with. For a long time, I believed that I'd been strong enough to beat the addiction on my own, so why would I sign up for meetings with some god-bothering group of losers if I'd still need to be going back there in eight years' time? I'd always thought I could fight it on my own. After all, I was the best fighter I knew. I was scared of nothing and nobody. I could not be beaten. I was Shinny the invincible.

Except now, I wasn't. The best way to describe it is that I was sick and tired of being sick and tired. I was exhausted from always having to be fighting something, from battling with my demons. I simply wasn't strong enough to do it anymore. I was too tired to fight my addiction. I was too tired to fight the kid's mams. I was too tired to keep my business up and running, to make sure the bills were paid and keep a roof above my head. I was fucked. Finished. I'd had enough. I had no more fight left in me.

Looking back, Becky and Ashley stopping me from seeing the kids was the only way to get through to me, because that was what it took for me to realise that I was beaten. My one, fragile finger-hold on normal life had been taken away from me. I could no longer kid myself that I'd got a grip on my life. After 25 years of absolute chaos and mayhem, fighting every day to keep a hold on my sanity, fighting to satisfy my delicate ego, my disease had finally beaten me. Addiction had kicked the fuck out of me and I'd finally had enough. I threw in the towel.

It was then that I learned that you have to surrender to the illness in order to beat it. If you try to fight it, addiction will always win.

In surrender, I found sobriety. I lost, and it's the best thing that ever happened to me.

Puzzle piece 23

As we discussed before, dopamine and memory go hand in hand. We wonder how James experiences severe withdrawal symptoms, but they suddenly switch off when he gets his own way. The continuous memory of drug-induced happiness in the hippocampus pushes dopamine throughout the brain. This would give an intense feeling of pleasure whenever he sees drugs or alcohol, calming the severe side effects of the withdrawals. At this point, his drug and alcohol intake was not to ease the bad thoughts but to stop the intense withdrawal symptoms.

PART 4.

Recovering Out Loud

CHAPTER 24.

BREAKING THE STIGMA

I guess it's time I made a confession. Over the years I've become a bit uncomfortable with the term 'addict'. I understand the word accurately describes someone suffering with the darker consequences of the condition. And I completely accept that I was, by definition, an addict. However, I'm increasingly reluctant to use the word 'addict' when speaking about people who have left their destructive behaviours behind. The word 'addict' does nothing to credit or describe those who have changed their ways and harnessed their compulsions to put them to work for good.

Forever labelling people addicts is like punishing them for their sins of the past, despite how successful, restrained, helpful or productive they behave when they use their passion positively. Labelling us as addicts forever deprives us of hope and of the accomplishments we have achieved, as if we're bad no matter what we do. Surely conducting our lives in a manner that isn't damaged by addictive behaviours should afford us the right to drop the guilt-laden label? Otherwise, by that account, most of the people reading this book would still need to be labelled as 'bed-wetters'. You don't wet the bed anymore, presumably, but you once did in the past, so you're still a bedwetter today, supposedly.

I say we stop calling it addiction unless the person's behaviour is having negative consequences. Perhaps we should call the condition an affliction? Maybe we should sometimes even call it a gift? After all, our compulsions for excessive behaviour can often be used positively. This seems fairer and more accurate than simply labelling us with what is universally considered a negative term - 'addict'. After all, there are people with the same compulsive afflictions who have excelled in their field and never had a problem with drink or drugs in their life. Are they addicts too?

People in recovery are told that it's called alcohol-IS-m, as opposed to alcohol-WAS-m, because the affliction is something which has the constant potential to destroy our lives, whether we're currently drinking or not. And while I can see their point, I can't help but think that those who manage to shift their focus away from drink (or drugs or whatever) to something more positive deserve a different label. Surely if you focus your efforts into doing something productive, instead of feeding the demon disease, that's a good thing?

It reminds me a lot of the popular legend, a story I heard years ago about an old man who is teaching his grandson about life:

"There is a constant battle going on inside me," the old man said to the boy.

"It is a terrible fight between two wolves. One wolf is evil. He is my anger, envy, sorrow, regret, greed, arrogance, self-pity, guilt, resentment, inferiority, lies, false pride, superiority, and ego."

He continued, "The other wolf is good. He is my joy, peace, love, hope, serenity, humility, kindness, benevolence, empathy, generosity, truth, compassion, and faith."

"The same fight is going on inside you, and inside every other person, too."

The grandson thought about it for a minute and then asked, "Grandfather, which wolf will win?"

The old man replies, "Whichever wolf you feed."

The affliction we are talking about needs feeding. What it grows into depends on what you feed it, but you need to know that whatever you feed it, the affliction will grow into something extreme. Feed it with positive things and you can excel at anything you choose. Feed it with negative influences and you will end up fucked up, in jail, institutionalised, or dead.

If you remove 'alcohol' from the word 'alcoholism' you're left with '-ism'. And it is this 'ism' which I feel is the significant part of the compulsions which drive so-called addicts to behave as they do. I think of the ism as an 'Internal Spiritual Malady' which compels you to act in extreme ways. If you remove alcohol from your life, you're left with just the 'ism'. It's then up to you to decide what you will do with your 'ism'. Whatever you do, it will likely be done to the extreme, and that's why I believe recovered alcoholics and drug addicts are better described as extreme-ists, rather than addicts.

Observe any extreme-ist and they'll amaze you in one way or another. Their ability to focus and dedicate themselves is phenomenal. Their ability to achieve what they want to achieve, whether good or bad, is often beyond belief. They seem to be able to go the extra mile and work a little bit harder than most people. Surely the stigma that follows an addict after their recovery does them little credit at all.

And let's not forget that it all starts in childhood. It begins when children are developing their self-awareness. It's when children and teenagers are at their most vulnerable that they start feeding the wolves inside them. It's vital we help them to feed the right wolf. Otherwise, the results are catastrophic for those with extreme-ism tendencies.

It doesn't have to be that way though. With the right help and guidance, kids with these tendencies can grow to be superheroes, rather than be ravaged by compulsions they don't know what to do with at such a tender age. Kids looking for their place in the world look to adults as role models. They tune in to meaningful music for direction, watch films for cues on how to be cool, even though they're still just children and not yet wise enough to know what's good for them and what's so fucked they should run away quickly. They're too young to know better, but they're learning all they can from whoever they can anyway.

Surely we should be helping these kids. We should be helping all kids to avoid fucking themselves up, but those with extreme-ism tendencies need guidance more than most. Because left to their own devices, many of them will become addicts.

I believe that if we can recognise kids with extreme-ism tendencies early enough, treat them with compassion and love, and then help them to channel their compulsive behaviour into something positive, then we have the potential to nurture a generation of super-human beings. It won't always be a perfect journey, but we've got to fucking help these kids grow into something awesome and realise their amazing potential. After all, it has been proven time after time that if you harness that superpower, you can achieve greatness. I can't imagine why society wouldn't want to do that.

It's not going to be easy, but nothing worth having ever is.

Puzzle piece 24

Extreme-ism is based on the concept of motivational imbalance, which signals the need to gain superiority and overrule basic concerns. There are different extreme-isms that relate to the same psychological nucleus. Those of which, we have all seen in James throughout his journey, including extreme infatuations, diverse addictions, and, of course, violent extreme-ism. James showed both extreme and moderate tendencies, allowing him to be completely irrational but at the same time completely sane.

CHAPTER 25.

SHITTY LITTLE BABY STEPS

It would be impossible to identify the moment when I stopped being an addict and considered myself recovered, so I won't even try. The story of my recovery weaves in and out of my life's stories about boxing, and relationships and bands and children and everything else that happened in my crazy life. I can hardly remember all of it myself, and writing this book has been difficult. I simply can't remember everything or the order it all happened. But what I can do is describe the journey, the important stages and how the road to recovery is a slippery and treacherous path to be on. My journey as told here essentially starts with a trip to my doctor, but really, it began with me drinking from a puddle.

To the untrained eye my road to recovery was rocky and peppered with failures. And that's true. It might be that the number of times I've got clean and then relapsed casts a shadow across any recovery success I might currently be enjoying. If I've relapsed so many times previously, what makes me think this time is any different? How can I even call my dubious track record a success at all? Am I still an addict waiting to relapse?

To answer that question you have to see my journey through the eyes of an addict. Every addict who is using, getting clean, relapsing or recovering (that's all of us, then!) – every one of us is on a journey. You might be taking the first tentative steps on the journey to recovery, or you could be stumbling along, making mistakes and relapsing. Or, you could be like me, working so hard on the recovery process that I feel strong enough to cope with whatever my addiction might throw at me – right now at least.

The journey we are on is one of learning, discovery and self knowledge. It's a journey which most people never attempt to undertake, and by that I don't mean just addicts – I mean everyone. Most people are bumbling through their lives, hoping they're wise to keep themselves sane and functional. They do their best with the knowledge they have.

Thankfully, most people don't face the same challenges we addicts do, and so they don't fall as hard or as far when the shit hits the fan. As recovering addicts, we have to be on our A-game all the time. We have to be constantly learning about ourselves and finding new ways to keep our disease at bay. It's a process of self-awareness and personal development that begins in the darkest recesses of hell, but if you work at it, the process can lead to dizzying heights of success. As extreme-ists, we can make miracles happen with our dedication and persistence. Recovery and personal development is a reward worth working for, believe me.

My journey to recovery began around 10 years after I started using cocaine. In that time I'd already fucked up my life countless times and I could see I had a problem just by looking around me. Few people were using drink and drugs like I was. I used these substances aggressively. For me, it couldn't be just a couple of beers and a few lines. Once I started, the slightest sniff and I was off on a downhill journey which would inevitably lead to chaos of some sort.

I watched other people having a good time and saw that they could finish their drinking and drug use, and then go home and continue their lives relatively normally, whereas I would always go ten steps further. I'd be drinking more and still drinking long after everyone else had gone home. I just couldn't stop until I was the last man standing. It was the same with my drug intake. Whatever it was, I'd take more and be still going long after everyone else had passed out. It was an obsession. It was a compulsion. It was as if I was possessed and I simply Could. Not. Stop.

As I say, I did things differently, and noticing that difference made me realise I had a problem. I'd also put two-and-two together and realised that the major problems in my life had been caused by my addiction. I'd ruined my schooling, fucked up relationships, created a violent persona that had become my identity – all as a result of my dependence on drink and drugs. And, worst of all, I'd fucked things up for my children. I knew that I loved them more than anything I could imagine, but even knowing I had this responsibility, I still could not stay clean. I knew then that I was fucked.

There was a battle going on inside me where I knew I was doing wrong, but I loved the buzz so much I couldn't stop myself from doing it. I'd also built an identity as a hard-partying, womanising, drug dealing, violent gym freak, and changing that would mean changing the very essence of who I was. My image and my behaviour protected me from bullies and stopped me being so frightened, scared, and I couldn't risk letting go of that protection. I couldn't risk dropping my guard. I knew it was fucked up, but I had no idea how to stop it.

I'd quit and got clean under my own steam a few times. I'd succeed and stop for a while, but inevitably I'd relapse and go right back to the beginning. I'd made promises I didn't keep both to myself and to the people I loved. I tried so hard to quit, I really did, but I just couldn't do it. I'd tried setting boundaries for my drinking and drug use – only drinking at the weekend (failed), only drinking once a month (failed), only drinking at family parties (failed). I was, stupidly, looking for a way to quit a little, but still enjoy the buzz sometimes. I tried to outsmart a problem that was way smarter than I am.

Like I said at the beginning of this chapter, to the untrained eye, my story might look like a failure. In reality, before I even sought help I'd already taken the first steps on the road to recovery. We all know that the first stage is to admit that you have a problem, and I'd done that, but what I am referring to here is the start of my recovery education. I'd begun to start thinking about how I might beat the disease, and I was taking steps to get clean. They were clumsy, ineffective, shitty little baby steps, but I was finally moving, creeping, in the right direction. I'd started to learn.

Every learning process begins by being crap at something. For example, when you first started learning to drive, you were crap at it. When you first started to walk, you were crap at it. If you learn how to play the guitar, you'll be crap at it at first. That's just the way it goes. Get used to it. Realise that you know fuck all about recovery. You're a rookie. There's so much you need to know, and you're just starting out.

The car-driving analogy is an especially good one because it helps to illustrate the four stages of learning. These are:

- Unconscious incompetence

- Conscious incompetence

- Conscious competence

- Unconscious competence

When you start to learn how to drive, you can't yet drive, and you don't even know what to do to start driving properly. You're incompetent, and you don't even know how incompetent you are. You're 'unconsciously incompetent'. You're shit, and you don't even know you're shit.

Then as you take a few lessons, your instructor will show you what you should be doing. At this stage, you still can't drive, but at least you're starting to understand what you need to do. You're 'consciously incompetent'. You're still shit at it, but now at least you know why you're shit at it.

Then, after a few more lessons, you're starting to get the hang of driving. You can drive, but you have to concentrate. You're 'consciously competent'. You can do it, but you have to think about it constantly, or you fuck it up.

Eventually, you've been driving for so long that you don't even have to think about it. It just happens automatically. You know what

MAKING OF AN ADDICT

to do and you can do it without thinking. You're 'unconsciously competent'. You can now say that you drive.

But here's the but – and it's a big but. Sooner or later, if you don't pay enough attention, you will fuck it up and crash. You are, in fact, always learning, and you should always pay attention to the road you're on. Otherwise, you'll crash and burn. And people do. Regularly.

I've said it before and I'll say it again – addiction is a thinking problem. Addiction is cleverer than you are, and it's always thinking of new ways to get you. You might learn a little, and you'll think you have it beaten, but if you don't keep working at it the addiction will get cleverer and stronger, and it will come back and fuck you up even harder.

Addiction is a progressive disease. It doesn't get weaker as you stay sober for longer. It keeps growing, getting smarter and tougher. So that's what you need to do as well. Start your learning process now. At first your progress will be slow and shitty. You'll fail and fuck things up. But the more you learn the stronger you'll get. And the stronger you get the more likely you are to stay clean and sober.

As you stay sober you need to remember that your disease is growing, and so must you. You must keep learning and growing stronger too.

Start your journey from wherever you are right now. Start thinking and learning. It's the only way to beat the demon.

Puzzle piece 25

We know that James has become a completely different person, and we wonder why he pretends to be calm and collected. Was James creating this character for offence or defence? Being bullied as a child can definitely scare you into never wanting to feel so hurt and vulnerable again.

As he grew up he realised if people were wary and cautious, it would shield him from the potential pain he already endured as a child. James created this alternate version of himself as he felt he could not truly be himself in fear of being judged, restrained and humiliated.

CHAPTER 26.

BUCKLE UP

Buckle up folks, because it's going to be a bumpy ride. I'm sorry, but if you bought this book looking for a quick fix or a silver bullet to cure addiction, this ain't it. Here it is in a nutshell – it's going to be hard work. It involves laying your soul bare and admitting to every mistake, character flaw and fucked up and degrading thing you've ever done. And that's just the start.

Recovery is going to be the hardest thing you have ever attempted. It involves a level of learning and self-scrutiny far more taxing than any schooling or education you went through. Yeah, if you're a quantum physicist you might be smart, but try learning about a subject while you're having the legs kicked out from under you, while you undergo a character assassination that highlights your every fault. No, recovery doesn't happen at the flick of a switch. It's fucking agony — a slow, heart-breaking agony, and it only works if you put in enough effort. But fuck me, it's worth it, I swear.

Your effort is the key to recovery success. Your willingness to do what needs to be done, whatever the cost, is what will determine ultimate success or failure. I know it sounds like a mountain to climb but, believe it or not, you do have what it takes to make it happen. To paraphrase Canadian clinical psychologist Jordan Peterson, life is hard work. Everyone you know, everyone on the planet, is suffering or has suffered devastating disasters at some point in their life, and often several of them. All of us have suffered, and the suffering will likely continue to some degree or in some way or another. Life's not easy. Nobody's life is free of suffering. There's no getting away from that fact.

But here's the good news. You are stronger and more capable than you think. That's not psycho-babble. That's a fact. And it applies to you as much as it does anyone. People all over the world face enormous suffering and hardships, and they keep on going. You can do it. I swear you can. But you have to be willing to work your fucking arse off for it. If you turn around and face the suffering voluntarily, you will find out that you are way tougher than you think. You may not believe it now, but if you have a compelling purpose and are willing to face the challenges head on, you absolutely have what it takes.

It's impossible to create a life which is without hardship and challenges. You will inevitably face disasters of one kind or another. But if you have a compelling purpose, if you are willing to tackle the challenge, if you are willing to do what it takes and fight hard, you are tough enough to overcome it.

I promise you that this is true. I'm only one man, but millions like me have done just this, and some of them were in a way worse state than you. They succeeded anyway.

You, my friend, can do this.

Puzzle piece 26

As James said before, addiction is now known as a disease within the mind. Although addictions are treatable, there generally isn't a cure, but they can be successfully managed. Relapse is a possibility and as James expresses it is hard to overcome. Research shows that combining medicines and therapy is the best chance for success. This is why today James believes anyone can do it if they receive the right support.

CHAPTER 27.

THE BASEMENT

It's almost embarrassing now, to admit that I thought I could beat addiction through sheer willpower alone. The disease had proven on numerous occasions that it could easily kick my ass and defeat my attempts. I should have known that I wouldn't be able to kick the habit alone, but I knew so little back then.

Unfortunately, I didn't have anyone to turn to for help in those early days. I didn't know anyone in recovery and wasn't even aware that there were dedicated recovery services. Even the people around me couldn't help. Most of them thought I was a raving lunatic and wouldn't have dared to step in and suggest that I needed help. I was a fucking head-the-ball and nobody would want to take the risk of pissing me off.

Only my sister, Gillian, was brave enough to tell me what a bell-end I was. She was fiercely protective of my mother and knew about all my manipulative behaviour. Despite how badly I treated her, mam could only see me as her blue-eyed boy who was a bit of a rogue, but wasn't a monster like everyone said I was. She said I was an "angel with a dirty face". My sister knew otherwise and saw me for what I was. She wasn't at all frightened of me and frequently gave it to me both barrels. She'd call me a 'no-good bastard' and I fucking hated her for it. If anyone else spoke to me the way she did there would have been blood, but she got away with it because she's my sister. She was the only person to ever confront me head on about my destructive behaviour, and I respect her highly for that.

One of the main reasons nobody could help me is because I didn't listen to anyone. Nobody had control over me as far as I was concerned– not my family, not my partners, not my friends, the police, the government. Nobody.

Me and my great big fucking ego. We always knew best.

Becky couldn't help me. She and I had countless arguments about my drink and drug abuse, and I made endless promises that I would sort myself out, but it never happened. I'd stay clean for a few weeks before losing the battle with my ever-more determined disease. She, like me, had no idea what to do, how to help or where to turn for guidance. Neither one of us had a fucking clue, so we just argued about it. That was our life. Arguing and fighting, because neither of us knew any better.

Ashley couldn't help me either. She was probably the most civilised person I'd ever known at the time, but was so far out of her comfort zone with me she had no idea what to do. While we would often argue, Ashley and I would also sometimes sit down and have sensible conversations about what we might do about the situation we found ourselves in. In the end, knowing there was nothing she could do to stop me from being me, she realised the only option she had was to protect our precious baby.

By the time I'd decided I needed some proper help I was certainly conscious of the fact that I had a problem, but I can't say I was always that fussed about sorting it out. This was the height of my party days and, while I knew it was fucked up, I shielded myself from admitting it fully, because to do so would be to admit that I was a bit of a cunt. The fragile, frightened boy in me simply couldn't face that admission of guilt.

However, I did go to my doctor to find out what help was available for people like me, who had a little bit of a problem with the old drink and drugs. He referred me to a local government-run service called The Basement – quite an ironic name for a facility which catered for people at rock bottom. It was the place where addicts would go to exchange needles and get doses of the heroin substitute, methadone. When I got there I looked around at the down and out wasters who frequented the place and thought "Fucking hell, I don't belong here. I'm not like them. I'm different. I shouldn't be here. I'm better than this!"

How fucking wrong I was.

It would be a while before I could compare my problems to those I saw at The Basement. At the time I thought I was different because I was just about holding my life together. I thought I didn't belong there because I wasn't sleeping on the streets. I thought I was different because I had a job, a relationship and a house. I thought I was different because I kept myself clean and didn't smell like shit. I saw so many differences, but what I was missing was that there were also a lot of similarities. I just didn't want to see them.

This is something I would urge you to do if you think you need help with addiction. Don't think you're different or above those who have ended up totally down and out. It's more useful to look at the similarities, to understand how you might benefit from the help available to stop you becoming more fucked up than you are now. If you have a drink or drugs problem, you have a lot in common with them, believe me.

Despite feeling a bit high and mighty about The Basement, I did give the programme a go. Part of the treatment consisted of using something called a 'black box' which delivered small electrical shocks to your ears or ankles. The idea was that the shocks would re-establish your natural dopamine system which had been dulled by drink and drugs. Dopamine has a major role in how your body interprets pleasure and, when you're getting your kicks from drink and drugs, your body's natural dopamine system gets inhibited.

And it worked, a little– kind of. I certainly got a bit of a kick from using the black box treatment and I did get clean for a few months. Really, though, it was a bit of a piss-poor treatment for a dedicated addict like me. There was no way a few gentle tingles from a black box were going to stop my disease. I was clean for a while, and even got back to training and eating healthy, but at the first opportunity the mask slipped and I was back to the mayhem.

I can't remember what it was that finally broke me, but I'm certain it would have been some kind of stress, coupled with an opportunity for me to drink and use. I'd have thought that I was clean enough and strong enough to have just one or two, and then stop. I was so naïve I thought I had it sorted. I honestly thought I was never going to drink again. I'd promised Becky I'd stay clean and, at the time, I honestly believe I meant it. But of course, I was weak and easily beaten. I hadn't yet done the work I needed to do.

My relapse was quite something. It always was. Each time I got clean I'd think that I'd finally got enough power in me to beat it, but the disease keeps coming back stronger every time, and the eventual relapse gets more destructive with it.

I think all addicts go through this cycle and this delusion of thinking we have the disease at bay, thinking we are strong enough, wise enough and resilient enough to stay clean, even though we haven't understood our situation. If we're not strong and haven't worked hard at understanding our addiction, we haven't got any defence when the disease decides to take us back.

Stopping is easy. Staying stopped is much, much more difficult, and a few electric shocks weren't anywhere near enough to keep me clean and dry.

PUZZLE PIECE 27

James became unpredictable, paranoid and confrontational, deterring people from approaching him especially when it came to the subject regarding his drug addiction. It is possible that people around him were unintentional enablers; this behaviour could have allowed James to continue a self-destructive pattern. It is difficult to talk to someone with an addiction, especially for a loved one. More often than not, pushing an addict towards recovery can be seen by them as judgement, resulting in destructive behaviour.

CHAPTER 28.

Fuck this shit

I spent a long time as an addict thinking that I was unique. I'd seen plenty of dropout junkies and alcoholics who had gone completely off the rails with no dignity or hope left in them, the people who couldn't hold down a job or get themselves clean enough to have any kind of normal life. I wasn't one of those people. I still earned a living, I could socialise with relatively normal people and I was still desirable enough to attract beautiful, accomplished women to have a relationship with me. I wasn't down and out by any means. I was close, but I was still in the 'normal life' game, hanging on by my fingernails.

In my circle of friends and acquaintances I didn't know anyone who could help me with my problem. Yes, I knew a few druggies and a few drunks too, but they weren't the kind of people you'd look to as a mentor or turn to for help. As far as I was concerned, I was on my own. After all, the one time I'd asked a professional for help they gave me a little black box which sent electric shocks to my ears. Help wasn't exactly forthcoming.

The one person I did know who offered some advice was a bloke called Adam. He was a crazy motherfucker, just like me, but it turned out that he was also attending Alcoholics Anonymous. I didn't know much about AA at the time and, on his advice, I decided to give it a whirl, assured that attending meetings was a sure-fire way to get clean and well. I arranged to pick him up the next day and drive us both to the venue where the meetings were being held.

I arrived bang on time to be greeted by Adam and a couple of his mates, all of them staggering and totally pissed up. I was flabbergasted and asked him what the fuck he was playing at because I thought we were supposed to be getting fucking sober! He assured me that AA would be cool with them being wasted, because while you're trying not to drink, you're allowed to attend the meetings even if you are pissed. This AA lark already sounded a bit fucking stupid to me, but I went along anyway to give it a shot.

The meeting was a fucking nightmare. In addition to Adam and his pissed-up mates, I ended up listening to story after story of fucked-up drunken arseholes. One bloke had burned his house down, almost killing his kids. Another was in and out of jail because of their drunken addicted behaviour. Another had been sober for 20 years but still struggled daily with the urge to drink. On and on and on. If this was what being in AA was like, it sounded hellish.

And then, when I heard a few of them start spouting off about God, I thought "fuck this shit!" I'd had enough. I honestly thought it was a cult, recruiting sad, fucked up people to become bible bashers. The meeting was confirmation that I was in this on my own. Nothing I'd tried and none of the help I'd received was working for me, so I'd fucking do it myself.

In reality, the meeting was typical of any AA meeting in the world and, if I'd been ready to listen, I would have found great benefit in hearing the experiences of the people there and the processes that they were going through. But I wasn't ready. I was a long, long way from being ready if the truth be told. I still thought I was capable, strong and up to the challenge of beating addiction myself. And, as usual, I was wrong.

It's often said that wise men learn from their mistakes. However, it's also true that wise men can learn even more from other people's mistakes. Me? I couldn't be taught anything. I wasn't ready and couldn't yet learn from my own fuck ups, let alone listen to others explaining theirs.

If you've been to AA and been disillusioned with it, my advice is to give it another go. The process is there to help and has proven to be enormously beneficial for millions of alcoholics all over the world. And it can help you too. You're no different from the millions who have been there before you. If you're not getting it, it's probably because you need to surrender yourself to the process and stop fighting it. You are not all-powerful. You've already proven that you can't do it alone. You don't have to believe in any religion or religious God to appreciate that you need help from a power greater than yourself. There's a lot AA can teach you.

I wouldn't be ready for AA for a few years yet, but I did know that I needed help, and the only option available to me was my doctor. By this point I'd heard about a drug called 'Antabuse' which is used to treat alcoholism by making the body extremely sensitive to ethanol– the alcohol found in beer, wines, spirits and the like. People who drink alcohol while taking Antabuse will suffer a very unpleasant reaction. And the more you drink, the worse the unpleasantness will be, including feeling sick, severe vomiting, headaches, chest pains, hyperventilation and breathing difficulties. In short, it's not fucking nice.

For me, Antabuse seemed to be the answer, at least for a while. According to the doctor, even a small amount of alcohol would knock me around pretty badly, or even kill me, and this was enough for me to put a hard rule in place – absolutely no fucking drinking. None. Zero. Never. That was the plan, anyway. Predictably, my disease had other ideas.

My band, Hanky Park, was in full flow at this point. I was gigging plenty, but while I was taking Antabuse the usual drink and drugs after the show were off limits. And it was all going pretty well too. I'd been off the gear and the drink for a few months and finding it pretty easy really. I was feeling strong and accomplished and, once again, I felt like I had the demon drink beaten. And once again, I was wrong.

All it took was one moment of weakness. One heady, excitable night when everything was buzzing and the good old crazy times were here again. Surely a shandy wouldn't hurt? Could it?

One taste of a beer was all it took, and I was back to being a raging alcoholic in the blink of an eye. One taste and the switch had been flicked. I wanted more and nothing could stop me. The crazy thing about it is, after avoiding drink because I was worried about the effects of Antabuse, when I did drink the Antabuse did fuck all.

Nothing.

I felt like I had won.

Within two days I was back to square one and drinking like I'd never been sober. And worst of all, I was loving every minute of it.

Puzzle piece 28

James' addiction overwhelmed everything around him whether that be responsibilities, relationships or help. An addict becomes selfish and self-centred. Characteristics of addiction can include being narcissistic, egocentric, self-absorbed and self-serving. Needs and desires become the priorities of his world.

Getting help was a positive start to his recovery, his self-centred ways had taken over once again. As James said he wasn't ready for AA, he didn't believe what he was hearing and that it could actually help. Drug abuse was at the forefront of his brain and negative emotions could have prevented James from feeling anything positive, experiencing only hopelessness and despair.

CHAPTER 29.

THE ORCHARD

Losing Becky and Donovan was certainly a major turning point in my addiction and recovery journey. I'd made promises I couldn't keep and bullshitted my way through the drama once too often, and I knew that I'd failed as a father. It was probably the first time that I realised I was beyond the point where willpower would work. I had no idea what help I needed or where to go to find it, but I understood my problem was greater than I could deal with alone.

That's not to say that I wasn't trying my hardest. Each time I promised to quit, I honestly meant it with all my heart. If I had taken a lie detector test at the time I would have passed, no worries. I really did want to quit. It's just that, at the time, I didn't know how to quit, and my promise would fade as my addiction fought back, inevitably ending in a relapse.

My conversations with my doctor weren't exactly ground-breaking, but they did at least open some doors and put me in touch with organisations that could possibly help – a revelation to me at the time because I had no idea that there was any suitable help out there. I was eventually put in touch with The Orchard in Salford which offered several different recovery and detox programmes.

MAKING OF AN ADDICT

The process began with Self Management And Recovery Training (SMART), a course designed to equip addicts with tools they could use to overcome cravings, along with a series of meetings along the general lines of an AA meeting, but not nearly as robust. This was my first glimpse of how behaviour change and talking about addiction could help with recovery, and I was optimistic about it – at first.

Unfortunately the programme isn't nearly robust enough to help a full-blown alcoholic like me. I'm sure it would help those who have a smaller demon, a less developed addiction problem, but for a hardcore alcoholic and drug addict like me it hardly scratched the surface.

Hardcore addicts don't just need to tweak their lifestyle. We need a full psychological re-boot. If you're a full-blown addict, lightweight courses such as SMART might help you to stop for a while, but they won't help you stay stopped. That said, if you're undertaking such a course it's well worth attending to take what you can from it. But if you're not tackling the root of the problem, your 'ism', then you're going to need higher-level help.

Predictably, for me, SMART didn't work, but it did help me to move forward in my recovery journey, and especially in listening to other addicts' experiences. I started to realise that there was some kind of magic to be absorbed from group meetings where people talked openly about their problems. It was a real step in the right direction considering where my head had been after my first AA meeting.

There is a remarkable power at work in group meetings, and the sooner you can recognise and appreciate this, the sooner you can start making significant progress towards understanding addiction and recovery. Meetings are one of the few places where you can learn a lot in a short time. Hearing other people describe their illness and their journey can help you to relate to your situation and your disease. Their stories can help you to understand yours.

It's all about peeling back the layers of your problem. It's like an onion. You have to get back to the core of the issue, and it's not going to be a quick or easy process. It'll take a lot of talking, listening to other people's stories, hearing about other people's recovery journeys, talking through the different layers of the ego, piece by piece, to understand what's happening to us. We have to get back to the core of how the problem started.

It's something I didn't get in the AA meeting I had been to previously, not because it wasn't there, but because I just didn't get it. When I went to my first AA meeting I honestly thought they would offer me a solution which meant I could drink, but not have a drink problem. I was looking for an easy fix, not a proper solution. Knowing what I know now I can see how ridiculous this was.

Having failed with SMART, The Orchard decided eventually that I was a candidate for detox, except this wasn't the kind of detox you might expect. The detox option offered to me was a home-based programme with a nurse who visits you in your home each morning. The first thing they do would be a breathalyser test to see if you'd been drinking, followed by the dispensing of pharmaceutical drugs such as Librium to take the edge off the symptoms of alcohol withdrawal. The nurse also provided vitamin supplements, which seemed as ridiculous to me at the time as it must to anyone reading this now.

The idea behind Librium is an interesting one. The symptoms of alcohol withdrawal are so severe that facing it without drug-assistance can be dangerous, risking potentially life-threatening seizures. Indeed, alcohol and heroin are, apparently, the only drugs from which cold-turkey withdrawal can be deadly. Cold-turkey is never pleasant, whatever your poison, but only with heroin and alcohol do you risk actually fucking dying. The fact that Librium calms the crawling delirium of withdrawal is an absolute godsend, and anyone who has ever tried cold-turkey will know how fucking hellish it can be. If you've been there, you know and if you don't then let me help you understand. Vomiting, diarrhoea, your legs can become so restless that people have been known to wedge themselves in a confined space to stop their legs moving, otherwise resembling something like the classic game buckaroo. Hot and stripping one minute and the next freezing cold. Severe headaches and an irritability so intense that any sound or word spoken out of turn can trigger an overwhelming burst of emotion. Imagine a new-born baby screaming because they are hungry and them not being fed... it's the same for an addict withdrawing.

Again, I stayed on the wagon for a few days before finding a way to fuck it up. That's how your brain works when you're in withdrawal. You trawl around your reasoning trying to find a shred of justification that will allow you to have a drink of some kind, and it can seem quite righteous and correct if you just squint a little and believe the bullshit you come up with. We addicts let our brains get away with some pretty ridiculous shit, just so we can talk ourselves into having a drink.

I had just a couple of cans... okay it was eight — I had eight cans, which was just a tiny little amount for me, pretty much nothing at all really, not a proper drink eh? Still, in the morning I had to do a breathalyser test, which, to my absolute amazement, I blew negative. I have no idea how I did it. Perhaps it's because I'm a big lad who can soak up eight cans and blow a zero on their stupid fucking test. Still, however it happened, it meant I lost all faith in the process and started drinking again in earnest. I can honestly say that all I got from the home-detox programme was disappointment and despair, and the soul-destroying knowledge that nothing was going to work.

Nevertheless, deep down, I knew I had to keep trying. So I kept on trying. The Orchard hit me with everything they had – meditation (which today is a big part of my recovery process), acupuncture (which gave me a bit of a buzz, but not much else) and the continuation of the SMART meetings (which were kinda useful, but inevitably too lightweight for my needs). And I kept doing what I did best, going at it great guns and full of hope before blowing out on a drink and drugs bender which put me back to square one. I kept on trying, and I kept on fucking it up.

Often the relapse happened simply because I was bored. When you've got nothing to do but think, that little crack-pipe eventually pops into your head. And once it's there, it starts to chip away, gradually getting bigger, and louder, and stronger, growing and growing until you simply can't ignore it anymore. And, eventually, you give in. If you're an addict without the knowledge and the strength to fight back, you'll always give in eventually. I didn't know how to deal with the creeping, growing, all-consuming addiction withdrawal rattle in any other way.

I remember performing gymnastic-style mental reasoning to justify my hit and find a way to make it happen. I remember telling Kat that I was just going to have a tiny bit of crack, you know, just to take the edge off. Of course, it turned into a full-blown bender. I'd try to convince Becky that I had walked to the all-night garage for a milkshake in the middle of the night when she found my muddy boots the morning after. I doubt she believed me. I even remember sneaking out of the house in the middle of the night with no shoes on so that I could go to a crack house and get hammered. I remember feeling really clever, that I had thought to go barefoot so that Kat wouldn't hear me clomping about. It wasn't until I turned up at the crack house with no shoes that I was brought down a peg or two. "Why don't you just carry your shoes with you until you're away from the house you dick head?" asked one of the crack-heads. I thought I was smart, but I was just a drug-addled moron.

Despite my devious, drug-fuelled behaviour, despite my lying and broken promises, despite my repeated failures, relapses and benders, despite all this, I really did want to quit. I tried everything I could to stop, but I couldn't do it alone, and it seemed that nobody could help me. And that's a fucking massive problem for addicts.

When an addict decides they're ready to stop we have a very small window in which to take action and get practical help. Unfortunately the systems we have in place are often fraught with delays. If you go to your doctor there are likely weeks of waiting until you finally get to speak to someone who might, just might, be able to help you. And, for the addict, that's simply too late. When we are ready to receive help we need to get that help right now. And if we don't get the help, it's too late. Then we get frustrated and distracted and we say "Well fuck it then!"

That's how, why and when relapses can happen.

Sadly, a lot of people die between the time they ask for help and when that help arrives.

Puzzle piece 29

Although James wanted to make a positive change, for his brain this wasn't an option. James entered a stage called relapse justification; this meant his brain was in fact telling him to do all the things he knew were wrong. For somebody whose brain was constantly stimulated with dopamine rushes, stopping would not have sat well.

Justifying his relapse was a way of trying to get the neurochemical reward that was associated with drugs. However, for James, and most people, relapse justification is a normal part of the process, and if we recognise these negative thoughts they can be combated.

CHAPTER 30.

SMITHFIELDS

I was essentially blagging my way through life. I was blagging my partners, making them believe that I was going to change. I was blagging friends and family with the same lies too. I was definitely blagging my way with my business, because I had no fucking clue how to run a business refurbishing bathrooms, kitchens and lofts. I'd hire professional fitters who knew what to do and blag my way through, pretending I was project managing the jobs. And I was definitely blagging myself, making me believe that I had my shit together enough to keep the show on the road and the wolf from the door. But deep down, I knew I was a mess. The business was going from bad to worse and eventually, the pressure built to unbearable levels. And, as we all know, stress is what sends addicts into a flat spin.

I was already drinking and using to excess, but somehow managed to wake up each morning and go to work, spending the day counting down the hours until I could have my first drink. I'd throw the first one down my neck as soon as work was done, trying my best to keep that threshold of staying sober during the working day. But come five o'clock and I had my first can, that would be me drinking for the night. The more stress that came my way, the more I drank, and the more I drank the worse I felt each morning.

The weekends were even worse. Between Friday afternoon and Monday morning I could easily smash 70 cans of beer, along with an impressive amount of wine and cider too. It was normal for me to spend the whole weekend pissed. Those Monday morning wake up alarms were getting harder and harder as each week went by.

I remember the first time I caved in and had a drink first thing in the morning. It was after a particularly heavy weekend of drinking and smoking crack, and I'd woken up feeling like absolute shit. It wasn't a new feeling but it had been getting worse for a while, and now it had reached the point where I simply could not function enough to get my act together. I knew that the only way to get me moving was to feed the addiction. I grabbed a can and downed it in one.

I can't tell you how blissful it was. It was 7.30am.

I remember thinking I'd found the cure for my lousy mornings and nightmarish days. If I just had a drink to calm my cravings first thing, I could get through the day and perform well enough to keep my business running. Looking back now, I realise that the drink had got me by the throat. From there it was an easy step to drinking a beer at intervals throughout the day to stop the itch. If something happened and I had some stress I'd wallop a can, and that would mean I could get through the shit and keep going. The drink became the solution for all of the problems I was experiencing. To me it felt good, but in reality I was in meltdown mode and this was classic alcoholism.

I spent months like this, drinking throughout the day and then filling my weekends with as much drink as I could get down me. I was also doing crack a couple of times a week at least. I still trained occasionally, doing the odd workout here and there, but again, I was blagging myself. I was so fucked my training was a waste of time and I'd put on so much weight I couldn't even pretend I was in shape anymore.

And then there were the night terrors. The need for drink had gotten so bad that I'd wake in the early hours sweating, spending the next few hours curled up in a ball with every muscle tensed and my jaw clenched, groaning in pain. The only thing that could cure the horror was to have a drink. It got so bad that when I went to bed I had to make sure I had a drink on the nightstand next to me so I could soothe the pain when I woke up in the night. On the rare occasions I did not have a drink ready for whatever reason, I'd try my hardest to endure the agony, white-knuckling my way through it until, eventually, inevitably, I'd call Kat to bring me some. By this time she and the kids had moved out, so I'd be on the phone, begging and pleading to her, screaming down the phone for her to come help me.

"I NEED A DRINK!" "HELP ME!"

"PLEASE HELP ME!" "PLEASE DON'T LEAVE ME!"

As soon as she turned into the driveway of my house I would feel a wave of relief come over me, and that first gulp of drink took all of the pain away. She was an angel, and that first drink was heaven. That woman was a lifeline for me and I'm sure I would have died without her.

But we all knew that I needed help.

One day, after one of my now regular calls begging to be saved, Kat drove me back to The Orchard to speak to my key-worker, Angela, who listened as I sobbed and explained my situation. Despite my failure to adhere to the home-detox programme, she made an appointment for me at a detox unit called Smithfields. I knew this was my only hope.

Smithfields is a residential unit with specialist detox facilities and a team of trained staff to help you through your stay. It's not a prison and you can leave at any time, but the week-long program is regimented and the full week of attendance is required and expected. By the time my admission date came around I was eager to get started and, after necking a few beers to prepare myself, I walked through the doors, ready to cure my addiction. There would be no more booze for a whole week.

The first three days involved massive injections of vitamins. These are not small injections of a few millilitres. These were great big painful barrel-loads pumped into your buttocks every morning for three days. They start you on Librium to avoid the inevitable seizures which accompany withdrawal, while all the time feeding you good wholesome food and providing a stress-free environment to ease you through the hard work and tough times to come.

Me? I treated it like a fucking holiday camp. I went from sobbing and begging for help, to being a cocky, obnoxious wanker within two days. I'd arse around, flirt with the girls, disrupt the group meetings and generally act like a twat the whole time. I'd even set up a little workout space in one corner of the communal area, leaning a couch against the wall to use as a punchbag. It was absolutely fucking ridiculous. I'd made a tiny amount of progress, but I thought I was back on my A-game and ready to get back in shape. I thought the whole thing was a big fucking joke.

Looking back I think I was doing my usual act of resisting any authority which could put my delicate ego in its place. Instead of doing as I was told and learning, I acted up and fucked around to hide the fact that I was frightened, and I got aggressive with anyone who challenged me about my behaviour.

And while all this was going on I was still trying to run what was left of my business at the same time. There I was, in a detox unit for acutely sick addicts, and I was arguing with builders and kitchen fitters over the phone in a bid to make sure I still had money coming in. I was on the phone one day, shouting and swearing when Louise, the manager of Smithfields, came over to tell me to be quiet. True to form I fucking lost it with her, told her to "Fuck off" and "Who the fuck do you think you're talking to?"

Understandably she was royally pissed off. She came right over to me and got in my face, telling me to shut the fuck up or else. This was like a red rag to a bull for me and I went ape-shit. So there we were, shouting and screaming at the top of our lungs until one or the other of us retreated to our room. I got called to the office less than an hour later, telling me that I was being kicked out and had to go home. It was day five of the prescribed seven.

Personally, I wasn't that bothered. I already felt much better and thought that I'd achieved everything which could be gained from the

Smithfields experience. I told Kat, Donovan and my mam that I was fixed, not to worry, and that I felt better than ever. They'd heard it all before, of course, but as far as I was concerned I was fine and I was never going to drink again. Fuck Smithfields, the cheeky bastards. Fuck them all.

I thought I was so special, when in reality, I was fucking nobody.

I was so brash and cock-sure that I even went back to the pub I'd been frequenting before my Smithfield detox. I was so sure I was cured I thought that going to a pub was no big deal. I could handle it. I didn't need to drink. And yes, I realise how fucking stupid that sounds now, but at the time I honestly thought I was indestructible. In my defence, I did need to go to the pub. The Royal in Farnworth was where all of the builders and fitters in the area met up to drink, so it was a good place to meet the people I needed to work for me in my business. For five days after my Smithfields exit I sat in that pub each evening drinking water, telling everyone who would listen how sober and fixed I was, bragging that I was never going to drink again.

But by this point, the illness had been craving drink for a whole ten days – the five I'd been in detox, and the five I'd spent abstaining after I left. And the illness, well it was hungry as fuck. On the surface I was doing well, and I really believed I was okay, but underneath it all I was sitting on a ticking time bomb. Eventually, predictably, I broke. It was just supposed to be one drink, but that's all it took to open the floodgates for my addiction to roll through and smother me like a tsunami. On the same night I picked up that drink, I followed it with another dozen. And before the night was through I was smoking crack again. From then on, I would be smoking crack every night for the next three months. It took just a few hours for me to go from seemingly recovered to being a raging addict again.

The amount of time I was able to stay off the drink and drugs was getting shorter and shorter as my addiction grew stronger and stronger. Each time I managed to find the strength and willpower to quit, the disease found a more convincing way to drag me back in again. It's like building a wall that gets knocked down by a car. So you build it back bigger, only for it to get knocked down by a van. So you build it back bigger, and along comes a bus. Each time you beat the illness it comes back bigger and stronger and more extreme than ever before. That's why addicts tend to go downhill further and further each time, with each relapse being more and more extreme and fucked up than the last. When you think you've been as low as you can go, the disease comes back with a new level of mayhem and destruction. Don't ever think you can't get any lower, because believe me you can.

I used to look at the people in Alcoholics Anonymous and Narcotics Anonymous meetings I'd been to and think "I'm not as fucked as them!" And while that was largely true at the time, what I hadn't understood was that I wasn't that fucked — yet!

I hadn't lost my job — yet.

I hadn't hospitalised my partner — yet. I hadn't attempted suicide — yet.

I hadn't burned my house down with my kids inside it — yet.

But all of these things were possible in the future if I didn't solve my addiction problem. The addiction will take you to places you never thought you could go. It will mess with your mind and make you do things you never thought you'd do. All of the things I thought I could never do, they were slowly one by one, becoming part of my life. Some of those things that previously I hadn't done yet, now I was doing them.

There are a lot of 'yet' scenarios and situations out there waiting for an addict, waiting for them to just get low enough, or desperate enough, or fucked up enough to consider them an option. Yesterday these things would have been horrific to think about, but today they can seem like a sensible, valid or inevitable option. Every 'yet' you've ever heard of or thought about, they're all out there, waiting for when the illness has destroyed us enough. Every 'yet' can come to pass if the disease is left to its own devices.

I spent three months drinking and smoking crack day and night, sinking lower and lower into my addiction, knowing that I had, once again, fucked up my best chance at getting my life together. The two group meetings a day at Smithfields hadn't registered enough to keep me sane or sober, but I still knew, deep down inside that these meetings were somehow the key to some kind of salvation. The problem was, I was on my own, with no guidance or mentor, no advice or any way to understand how best to use the opportunities that were being presented to me. I didn't understand the process or how to make it work. I was doomed to revert back to the only behaviours I knew because nobody had shown me a better way to be. It wasn't anyone else's fault. I just didn't know any better and wasn't clever enough to work it out for myself.

Puzzle piece 30

The functional addict in James made excuse after excuse in order to drink. Excuses were the highlight of James' life "I've worked all day, I deserve this" or "just one won't harm me, I'm recovered". The outward ability for James to maintain a normal life was coming to an end. Sooner or later, like all functioning addicts, he had to face the consequences that he managed to avoid for so long.

As we all know arrogance is considered to be one of the least attractive personality traits. James entered the program on a positive note, but, again, left feeling entitled and with the need to state his superiority. James believed that showing off would convince others how strong he was, but more often than not, had the opposite effect.

CHAPTER 31.

THE ONLY WAY OUT

Kat did her best to help me, but she had no idea what to do. We were still officially together, but she was gradually backing away, spending more time at her mum's and less time with me, while at the same time still supporting me financially.

By now my business had completely gone to shit and I was claiming sickness benefits. There was just no way I could hold down a job or run a business when my day was spent drinking. Kat, bless her soul, would do her best to support me. I knew she'd be there for me whatever happened, and I knew I could rely on her to bring me a drink when I needed one. She'd long since realised that refusing would only lead to me screaming in agony and pleading down the phone for her to "Help me, save me, please don't let me suffer." It's no wonder she did the only thing she could, even though we both knew that bringing me a drink wouldn't help in the long run. Even though she was there for me, it wasn't really a relationship anymore. Now she was more like my babysitter.

Three months of using led me right back to where I was when I entered Smithfields all those weeks ago, only now I was more desperate and hopeless. I had nothing. I wasn't allowed to see my children. I had no work. My relationship had gone to shit and my family were at their wit's end. I'd already begun to think about suicide, and the only thing that had stopped me doing so before now was my relationship with my kids. Now that I couldn't see them, as far as I was concerned I had only two choices – sort myself out or kill myself. I knew it was only a matter of time before I did the deed because the odds on me getting sorted were seemingly zero.

Previously the chance of going to detox had been a beacon of hope, but I'd blown my chance at that when I fucked about and abused the people who were trying to help me during my last detox stint. One day, in the depths of despair, Kat arranged a meeting with Angela, my key worker at the Orchard to see if we could somehow have another attempt at detox. After smashing a few cans in the car park to prepare for the onslaught, the meeting went exactly as I expected.

I knew before we arrived that I'd burned that bridge, and Angela was understandably dismissive of my chances of getting another shot at it. You can't just decide to go back to detox and hope they'll give you another go at it. You can't just pop in for a bit of detox whenever you like. There are waiting lists that are months long, criteria you have to qualify, and then there's the wasting of taxpayers' money to consider. There's a process, and I wasn't a good candidate for such a valuable resource as a detox programme. Angela said she'd try, but she wasn't hopeful. And to be honest, neither was I.

We all knew it was a waste of time trying. But both Kat and I could also see that, without help, I would be dead in a few months. I was going downhill fast. I could see where I was headed, and it frightened the shit out of me. I could tell it was all going bad in my head, and I told Kat as much. With nowhere left to turn for help it seemed my only option was to drink myself to death. What else could I do? I was a hopeless alcoholic and nothing was going to change that. While I didn't want to drink, I simply could not put it down.

It had reached the point where I couldn't do anything without beer. If I had to go somewhere I needed to be sure there was drink to be had, and if there wasn't, I'd have to take it with me. I remember I went to watch a mate who was running a marathon and, knowing I'd be out of the house and away from my booze for a few hours, I had to fill a rucksack with drink to keep me going. I carried alcohol with me like a life-saving medicine, even though I knew it was quite the opposite. But what other option did I have?

Less than a month after pleading with Angela for another chance at detox I was in a worse state than ever. Each morning seemed like a fight for my life. I had to get a drink down me as soon as possible because, if I didn't, the horror which came upon me was hell on earth. Without a drink I'd be dripping in sweat within the hour, my mind racing, my body tensed in agony and spasms. I'd be hallucinating, screaming for mercy, and it felt like the end of the world. I was broken with nowhere to turn for help. Nobody could save me now.

The more broken I became the more I knew that suicide was my only option. I knew without a doubt that I could not change and there was no help for me. I'd been in despair before, but now I was worse than ever. The state I was in was no good for my children. I knew they would be better off without me.

In the depths of my despair there were few people I felt I could turn to. After all, the state I was in there were few people who would or could help me. Kat was at the end of her tether, and my long-suffering mam had seen me fucked up and dying too often. I'd like to say I protected her from seeing how fucked up I was, but when you're at your lowest you can always rely on your mam. I knew she would always be there for me, so I'd call her up retching, crying, begging her for help. No mother can turn their back on that, so she'd come to my aid with the drink I needed. What else could she do?

PUZZLE PIECE 31

Kat and his mum had quickly become enablers, often supplying James with what he craved the most in order to stop the behaviour he was displaying. Enablers make excuses for their loved ones, excuses created from fear. The fear of losing James prioritised his needs over their own. Enablers are judged. However, when fear runs you, you are not yourself.

Despair caused James to act irrationally, screaming and shouting. He was as low as he could get and would do anything to stop how he felt, mainly when it came to withdrawals.

CHAPTER 32.

Do or die

My mam had seen me in some pretty desperate states before, but there must have been something even more distressing about the day in question. I'd called my mam with the usual chaos, begging her to save me, to bring me the drink I needed to stop the horror which had me by the throat. And she had come to my aid as usual and brought me the life-saving poison I needed. Watching me destroy myself must have been so awful that, the next thing I knew, we were in the car headed for The Orchard. To be honest, I hardly remember what had happened or how we came to be in the car, with me crying and shaking on the passenger seat. All I wanted in the whole world was to be put out of my misery. I just wanted to die.

I was in such an awful state that, this time, I hadn't called ahead to let Angela know we were coming. I simply turned up in reception with my mam and begged for mercy, screaming for Angela to help me. Angela must have heard me from her office because she came out and ushered me and mam to a consultation room, where I pleaded with her to take me back into the programme and help me. I was on my knees, sobbing, begging for her forgiveness, her mercy, her help. I told her that I knew I would be dead soon, either killed by drink or by my own hand if she did not help me. "Help me," I begged, "or I know I will cut my own throat."

At that, my mam went into shock, collapsing to the floor, gulping in enormous, soul-destroying sobs. Watching your formerly big, strong son begging for his life was simply too much for her to take. She'd seen me in some states, but nothing like this. Now she knew that I was about to end my life. I'd destroyed myself and everyone was better off without me, and I was destroying my mam too. Her heart was torn to shreds, and I couldn't do a thing about it.

And then, to my surprise, Angela broke. I doubt it was my desperation which affected her so much, but more likely the horrific situation I'd pushed my mother to endure. This professional woman who had seen it all was in tears now too, doing her best to look after my mam. My chaos was destroying everyone who came near me.

Once the situation had calmed a little, Angela left the room, promising to return in a few minutes. The minutes passed and felt like hours, my life hanging in the balance for what seemed like days until Angela came back into the room. I don't know who she talked to, what she did, or what strings she pulled, but somehow she had found a way for me to get back into detox.

Somehow, I'd been offered a lifeline – a two-week detox programme at The Sanctuary.

"Listen to me now," she said sternly, "and listen to me good."

"You cannot let me down this time. You cannot mess this up. I have moved mountains to make this happen for you. If you mess this up, I have no more power to help. Mess this up and I cannot help you again."

"Do you understand me?"

What Angela had achieved for me was unheard of. Most people wait six months, sometimes up to a year, for a place at Smithfields. I was checking in within a week. I knew I could not fuck it up. I had to face the manager, Louise, who I'd abused and threatened during my last visit, but apologising wasn't even difficult. I knew what I had to do. With my tail between my legs I had no pride left to lose, and I knew this was my last chance. And I was, truly, very sorry.

Although I was determined to make it work, it won't surprise anyone to know that I turned up at Smithfield's smashed out of my face. Kat drove me there, and by the time we turned into the carpark I'd already necked 12 cans, a bottle of wine and two big bottles of cider. My appointment was at 10.30 am. Even as I was checking in, I excused myself on a couple of occasions so I could go back to Kat's car and throw a can down my neck. I knew that this would be the last time I could drink and I wanted to be sure I'd drunk as much as I could. My disease wasn't going down without a fight.

Despite having been through it all before and knowing what to expect, the first few days at Smithfield's were a fucking nightmare. Within a few hours the withdrawal symptoms were upon me and I felt like I was going to die, and I remember thinking, "If I'm going to die anyway, I may as well drink myself to death." My brain was already scheming a way to get me back to drinking. I'm not sure if the Librium helped at all, but if that's what it felt like when the drugs are helping, I never want to go through withdrawal without them.

Thankfully the medication they provided at the end of the day helped me to sleep, but the morning after was even worse than the day before. Where I'd normally have a couple of beers on hand to take the pain away, here I was suffering every moment of my withdrawal. From what I could tell, the medication was doing fuck all to help me and I just wanted to die.

And, of course, all the time my demon disease was plotting. The diseased part of my brain was trying to conjure up ways to get drink in, or for me to sneak out and have a drink without jeopardising my place in the recovery programme. That sneaky bastard came up with thousands of plans, but each time, just at the point where I was ready to snap, my sensible brain kicked in. Instead of letting my crazy brain take over, this time, my sensible brain fought back. Above all else, despite the cravings, the withdrawal, the agony, I knew I could not fuck it up this time. I knew this was my last chance. I knew that failing would kill me. I knew I had to surrender myself to the programme and the recovery process. This time, I couldn't, wouldn't give in to my disease. I had to fight back. And that's exactly what I did.

Instead of pouring my extreme-ism into finding a way to drink, I became obsessive about giving my all to my recovery. I became extreme at getting clean. I went to every meeting I possibly could, followed every bit of advice I was given, I listened, learned, read and obeyed every part of the course. I wasn't just going through the motions like last time, doing the minimum possible to get through. I was there to do a job, and this time I was all in.

It was during the peer support meetings that I found the real magic that makes the recovery process work. During my last detox attempt I'd seen glimpses of it, but now, when I was giving my all, the magic from the meetings shone like a beacon. I knew there was real power in the process. I knew what I had to do. I had to shut the fuck up and listen. I took the cotton wool out of my ears and put it in my mouth. And when I did, I found that I could identify with the people talking. Their situations and woes often sounded so familiar. I heard myself saying to myself, "Fucking hell! I'm one of you!"

As the days went by the horror of withdrawal receded and I started to feel well. It must be amazing to someone who sees such recovery for the first time, how an alcoholic can go from death's door one day to seeming relatively well just a few days later. By day four I was playing my guitar and writing new songs – something I didn't think was possible without the help of drink or drugs. I was amazed at how creative I could be by just being me, no drink or drugs required.

I started training again too, revelling in the feeling of euphoria, knowing that I was beyond the worst. And even the Librium was helping a little, taking the pain away and helping me to not only cope, but get back to normal and start to feel strong again.

The only downside of my two-week detox was the constant nagging by the regular visitors from Alcoholics Anonymous and Narcotics Anonymous. I didn't trust them and I made it very clear that I didn't like those creepy bastards one fucking bit. To me, it felt like they were coming to our precious meetings to recruit people to their cult, to fill their heads with God bothering and sign you up for their cultish 12- step programme. Me? I wasn't fucking having it. Our peer support meetings were a vital lifeline and I did not want these shady wankers ruining it with their brainwashing and sinister motives.

I might have been in recovery, but I was still very paranoid.

After the two weeks were over I felt like a new man. The support available from Smithfields after the two-week detox was done worked wonders to keep me sober, and I attended their peer support meetings for many months afterwards. My recovery continued and the more meetings I attended, the stronger and stronger I became. But always, every meeting I went to, these knobs from AA and NA kept showing up, feeding people their bullshit. And eventually, I'd had enough.

"I know what you're fucking up to." I said one day, cornering the guy from Narcotics Anonymous as the meeting came to an end. "You fucking watch yourself ya cunt! I'm onto you fuckers. I'm not going to let you fuck this up for us, you and your fucking cult." He tried his best to convince me that I had the wrong end of the stick, that he was just trying to help people and in no way wanted to do anyone any harm. But I knew better. I was in recovery, but my disease was still paranoid. Physically I was doing ok, but mentally I was still not well in the head.

The next week they turned up mob-handed - five of them in total, and by this point, I'd had enough. Thankfully it didn't kick off, but I decided I was going to go and disrupt one of their meetings, just like they were doing to ours. I was going to tell them all exactly what I thought of them and what they should do. And if it kicked off, good fucking luck to them, because I would be more than happy to break all of their fucking faces.

Little did I know, but the meeting I turned up at was the nerve centre of Narcotics Anonymous in the North of England. There must have been 40 people in that room, and none of them seemed to be scared of me. As I sat down I contemplated what my next move would be, seething, agitated, with a big fat ego-chip on my shoulder. I'd fucking show them. I'd give them a piece of my mind. I would put them in their place.

Except, I didn't.

The longer I sat there and listened, the more their brainwashing seemed to work on me. Although, now I realised it wasn't brainwashing, it was magic. It was the same magic I'd experienced in the peer support meetings, but this time turned up to a thousand. The more I listened, the more my brain came to understand that I had them all wrong. In the heart of that meeting I realised – this was where I needed to be.

And then, something happened. A guy across the room started telling his story, and it was as if he knew me. He spoke my language. He told my story. He spoke about the violence, the sex, the drugs, the drink, the ruined relationships, the compulsive obsessions with anything his brain could latch onto. When he spoke, it was like I was talking to myself. I sank into my chair, processing what I had just experienced. And then it was my turn to speak.

"I came here tonight to pick a fight, but having listened to you I realise that I have found where I belong. I've been doing it wrong, and now I know that this is where I need to be."

From then on I became a regular at Narcotics Anonymous meetings. The man who shared his story became a friend, and I've told him many times that he saved my life that night.

Puzzle piece 32

Although the addiction had both a short- and long-term effect on James, it was evident he had put his mother into a devastating position causing severe emotional damage. His mother had witnessed him as he truly was. Shock can cause an individual to experience trauma or develop coping mechanisms such as co-dependent behaviours. Researchers have found that brains that have been harmed have the potential to unlearn addictive behaviours, while mindfulness and meditation can potentially lessen the risk of relapse.

CHAPTER 33.

CHRISTMAS NUMBER ONE

I threw myself entirely into the rehab process. It became clear to me why the people involved in Alcoholics Anonymous and Narcotics Anonymous were so evangelical about the meetings. After all, it's quite understandable that people who have found redemption after being so close to losing everything want to spread the word to others who are facing similar addictive demons. What seemed like a cult to me is more like a group of helpful people who want to help others to beat addiction. The recovery culture and community is passionate and committed and I had only been able to join it wholeheartedly once I was ready to understand it properly. And when I did, I was all in. I'd even signed up to do an eight-week course to get the necessary qualification so I could volunteer at Smithfields. Having been saved from the brink of death myself, I was eager to try to help someone else in the same position.

Alongside all this I was also throwing myself into my music. I'd previously thought substances were the key to being musically creative. After all, many of the artists I loved were notorious addicts – Jim Morrison, Bob Dylan and so on. For me, though, this couldn't be farther from the truth. Now that I was clean and sober my mind was ultra sharp. I'd woken up from the haze and was writing songs straight from the heart.

I was at a mate's house one day, Dave, a music producer I'd worked with previously, jamming and practising songs I'd written, ready to record demos of any songs that we thought could work. I was belting out one particular tune when his girlfriend came down the stairs and said: "That sounds like a Christmas song!"

At that moment, my brain seemed to jump into overdrive and I could see the future planned out ahead of me. Over the next few hours Dave and I came up with a plan for a hit record centred around how a bloke who had been in detox could recover and write a song that would be number one in the charts at Christmas. It was such an exciting idea and I could feel my extreme-ist tendencies swarming all over it.

The next few months were mental. We recorded the song, called it Christmas Number One, and started releasing snippets of it on social media. I used my skills of persuasion to get people to share it, and even roped in a few of the celebrities I knew to give it a mention on their social media channels too. The news of Shinny's Christmas Number One spread like wildfire and soon I had well-wishers from all over the country tuning in to see if we could pull it off. Could an addict just out of rehab really nail the number one slot for Christmas? We had just a few weeks to find out.

The real drive behind the plan was social media. I'd do a video every day explaining what we'd been up to, what kind of interest we'd had and what we were going to do next. And all the time the information about the song's success was punctuated with my story about what it's like to be an addict in recovery. I was still working hard at being clean and sober, still attending AA and NA fellowship meetings and volunteering at Smithfields, and people were fascinated by it all. It was probably the first time addiction and recovery had been spoken about so frankly and openly for anyone to hear. It's difficult to imagine, but the whole thing was like a movie plot unfolding. There was me, delivering daily live videos on Facebook, promoting Christmas Number One and talking about my journey to recovery.

Soon we were getting radio airplay when, one day, I got a call from the UK charts while I was doing a live video, asking me if I thought we could get a Christmas number one. "Too fucking right we can!" I replied, and everyone following me went wild! By now there were thousands of them, tuning in every day to hear the next chapter in the Christmas Number One story, and my step-by-step journey of recovery kept them coming back for more. This wasn't just about the song anymore. The recovery story was taking on a life of its own.

Eventually I got a call from Manchester's main radio station, Key 103, again coordinated to happen when I was live on air. We were chatting away about the record and how I was up against some big-name artists like Cliff Richard and Ed Sheeran. I was doing my best to be upbeat and positive, but there was no doubt that the DJ was taking the piss a bit and having a dig at my expense. When the call ended I was a bit fucked off.

My following was fucking livid too. Within minutes the Key 103 Facebook, Twitter, email, website – you name it, all of them were deluged with messages calling them out for how they had treated me on air. It went on for days, thousands of messages slagging them off for being so rude when all I wanted to do was spread a message of hope and good cheer. Eventually I got a call back from the DJ, apologising profusely.

From there, Key 103 got behind me and started to promote the record hard. It seemed to me like they realised they had got it wrong and underestimated the support I had behind me. They did what they had to do to get back on the right side, and it helped the campaign enormously. It wasn't long before I got asked to play at the station's annual Christmas gig at Manchester's MEN Arena, opening the show for none other than Robbie Williams.

From absolutely nothing and nowhere we'd started a movement that had disrupted the whole UK music scene in the run-up to Christmas. Fuelled only by my compulsive drive, with promotion solely via social media, we'd created a media sensation. When the Christmas chart rundown finally arrived we came in at number 24. We didn't get the number one spot, but we achieved something nobody thought could be possible. It was a wild time and our success had all come from the extreme-ist tendencies fuelled by my disease.

However, by January the buzz was over, and my disease needed something else to latch onto.

Puzzle piece 33

James was sober and in recovery. He began a new obsession; music. There has been evidence to suggest that as well as sedatives to relax, music has also been found to be as good at calming the nerves. Within James' recovery, he understood that his addictive personality was still present. He substituted one addiction for another in an attempt to compensate for what he lacked emotionally and psychologically.

CHAPTER 34.

Cyprus

Anti-climax doesn't even come close to how it felt when the Christmas Number One buzz was over. The self-seeking reward of having everyone's attention fed my addictive and compulsive tendencies, making me feel like I was famous, like everyone loved me. It felt just like the good old days during the rugby, the boxing and Hanky Park eras. And now all the hype was over and I came crashing back down to earth.

One good thing which did come out of it was that my following on Facebook stuck around and kept tuning in to my videos to find out how I was doing with my recovery. By now I was eight months sober and felt like I was well and truly recovered. I was doing pretty well in myself too. I felt happier, Kat and I were together again and I hadn't been drinking, using or shagging around for months. By the time my 40th birthday came about, Kat and I had booked a holiday to Cyprus to celebrate.

Recovering addicts will tell you that you need to watch out for triggers. I'd managed to deal with the triggers I encountered when I was back home in my normal life. I knew what to expect and had the knowledge, tools and experience to stop me turning to drink and drugs when those triggers occurred. I felt strong, and as we boarded the plane I felt in control of my drink and drug demons. Even after take-off as I watched the people in the seats nearby ordering drinks, I felt like I had it all under control. "At last," I thought, "I've got the bastard beat!"

My relapse started in the taxi on the way to our accommodation. I can't explain it fully but I felt something inside me switch, like a lightbulb coming on, and I knew I needed a drink. Perhaps it was being in a hot country, walking down the road past all those tempting bars with ice-cold beer on tap. Perhaps it was the rowdy partygoers who sounded like they were having so much fun. Perhaps it was just my own weakness simply compelling me to drink. Whatever it was, I could feel the disease gnawing away inside me.

Kat went pale when I told her how I was feeling and she urged me to call a friend from the fellowship. "You shouldn't have put yourself in such a tempting position while you're so vulnerable," he said. I hadn't felt vulnerable until the urges kicked in, so how could I have known this would happen? And regardless, it was done now and I needed help, sharpish. His suggestion was to have a nice cold can of Pepsi. Perhaps I was just dehydrated or needed a sugar fix? I did what he said, but I knew that Pepsi wasn't going to touch it. Even when I walked into the shop to buy the cola I could see the cans of beer in the fridge, dripping with condensation, and my addiction multiplied like a germ in a petri dish – growing larger, growing stronger by the minute.

Somehow I managed to convince Kat there wasn't a problem and we ended up in a bar, my brain turning somersaults trying to deal with the mayhem that was happening in my head. Every fibre of my being wanted a drink, but I knew if I gave in my disease would be all over me again. As the barman came to take our order I asked him for a pint, which he pulled and placed on the counter in front of me. I paid for it and watched as Kat walked out of the bar disgusted, hurt and frightened for what she knew would happen next. I stood there, staring at the foaming golden liquid in the glass for what felt like an eternity, before turning around and chasing after Kat, leaving the pint untouched where it stood.

I felt like a fucking superhero.

The next day went relatively smoothly, with only the occasional urge to grab a beer. I was distracted by how lovely it was to be on holiday with Kat, but I could still feel the disease picking at my mind. We enjoyed ourselves for most of the day before eventually ending up in a supermarket to grab some supplies on our way home. But as I walked past the fridge, the urge to drink took hold of me by the throat again. I calmly grabbed four cans of beer and placed them, without a hint of regret or drama, in the basket.

"What the fuck are you doing?" asked Kat, clearly panicked. "Don't worry about it," I replied, dismissively. "It's alright."

But quite clearly, it was not alright in the slightest.

As I got in the car I cracked a can and walloped it in one. "How do you feel?" Kat asked.

I paused a second, looking at the empty can.

"I'm alright," I replied. "But fuck me, I've missed that!"

And with that, the disease had got its claws into me once again. I felt a surge of energy coursing through my body as I opened the next can and downed it. And then the next. And the next.

Before I knew it, 20 cans later, I'd fallen into a drunken stupor in the apartment. And when I woke up the next day I did the same thing all over again. On the third day I woke up in the early hours, retching, spewing up bile and craving a drink with every nerve and sinew I possessed. I'd been sober for eight months, and it was less than 48 hours since I'd had my first drink and, already, I was suffering like a raging alcoholic – as if I had never been in recovery at all. That night I cried into Kat's lap as she held me, distraught and sobbing herself, both of us knowing where this would lead. And the disease did exactly what it is created to do. It destroyed me and my relationship all over again.

The next five days were spent drinking hard. I tried to convince myself and Kat that I could keep the drinking to be only to when I was on holiday, determined that I would not let the disease take hold again when I was back home. I promised her that as soon as we landed, that would be it. No more drinking. I was determined that I would not ruin my recovery. And I really meant it. I swear on my life, I really did mean it, but as the plane touched down and we cleared security I headed straight to the nearest shop and bought eight cans of lager to help make me calm enough to make it back home.

I didn't want the beer. I fucking needed it.

The fellowship meetings I'd been to had been powerful. I'd learned a lot by listening to other people's stories and it had helped me to understand my own journey into and out of addiction. However, I hadn't signed up for the 12-step programme for which AA is notorious and which makes it so successful. I was still resistant to the idea of having a greater power in my life. I was still resistant to the idea of a regimented, structured programme which I felt would limit my freedom and my capacity to be in control. I'd felt like I was strong and ready for anything, but compared with the disease that had been growing inside me, I was still weak.

We'd kept the disease entertained with the Christmas Number One and the attention of my following on Facebook, but once that buzz died down it needed something else. And, in going to Cyprus, I handed it to my disease on a plate. Addicts will tell you that it isn't the 20th drink that's the problem. It's the first drink that will fuck you up. There's no way back from that first drink – no way an addict can have one drink and then put it down and call it a day. One drink is all you need to open the door to let the devil back into your life. We have no strength to resist the effects of that first drink.

Puzzle piece 34

Relapse triggers are internal and external, these cause a person in recovery to crave and eventually relapse. James needed to understand the nature of his triggers in order to recover. Cyprus reminded James of his social, environmental and emotional past of drinking. Although this trigger did not force James to begin drinking while on holiday, it influenced the likelihood of alcohol misuse. The national institute on drug abuse reports that 40-60 per cent of people treated for substance abuse disorders relapse. James was exposed to the social cues that were holiday drinking, impacting his internal and external triggers.

CHAPTER 35.

CHASING THE DRAGON

The constant daily craving for drink and drugs was back and I felt like I'd never even been in recovery. The morning breakdowns, the night sweats, the retching, aching, screaming tension that can only be cured by giving in – it was all back and I was an alcoholic addict once again.

I came clean, not only to my NA support group but also to my followers on Facebook. The encouragement and support they gave me was humbling and inspiring, but the devil was out of the box and beating the shit out of me once again. I'd hoped that by owning the relapse, by admitting to it and making the efforts to get sorted, I hoped that would strengthen my determination and help me get back on track with my recovery programme, but it was no use. For weeks I was up and down like a yo-yo, one minute going hard at recovery, the next blowing out on a drinking bender or finding myself back at the crack house and off my face.

I'd become quite well known again by this point. The Christmas Number One and my social media notoriety had boosted my profile to the point where people were approaching me with collaborative business ideas. I'd brushed most of them off, but for some reason, one particular idea seemed to strike a chord with me. I don't know why. A mate of mine pitched the idea of a partnership in his micro-brewery project, launching an ale called Shinny's PMA – a Pale Manchester Ale. At the time it didn't occur to me that a brewery business might not be the most sensible idea for a recovering alcoholic. Of course, everyone around me saw what a fucking stupid idea it was.

Within weeks my mugshot was welcoming pub-goers from beermats and pump clip badges, winking and grinning my gold-toothed smile. What a fucking ridiculous joke! Obviously, I had to try the products we were selling and, all of a sudden, I was a real ale connoisseur! I'd be talking hops and wheat and barley, kidding myself that drinking a real ale wasn't the same as swilling lager as an alcoholic would. Not at all! This was different.

Yeah! 'Course it was! But inside me I knew different and I could feel the disease was more in control than ever. It felt violent, evil and all consuming.

Back at the crack house my addiction was moving up a gear too. There was no sense trying to kid myself that I was in recovery anymore. Recovery had quite obviously failed. You know your recovery has failed when you're an every-day regular at a crack house.

It seems strange to describe it as a normal day at a crack house, because that is a ridiculous statement in itself, but there was nothing at all unusual about the occasion in my mind. For me, it was perfectly normal. I'd been there for a while and we'd smoked all the stone we had in the house, so one of the lads went out to score some more. I stayed home with his girlfriend who, as usual, was smoking a bit of heroin while she waited, as you do. I'd tried smoking heroin before but it had been a bit half-arsed, to be honest. When you're coming down off crack you'll try anything to take the pain away, so I'd occasionally take a few weak toots of smack, but it wasn't really a proper hit. However, that night, as we waited for the fresh supply of crack to turn up, I asked his girlfriend to sort me out with a hit. So she did.

As the heroin burned, I took the foil tube between my lips and sucked in the smoke for all I was worth. It hit me hard, like the warmest, most loving cuddle your mother has ever given you. All of the pain went away and everything in my world was perfect. I was happy, blissful even. All of my woes disappeared as my body melted into a massive comfy cushion (that wasn't even there).

"You've had a proper hit tonight Shinny, love!" I heard the girl say before I blissed out into my own little world.

My life had been a living nightmare for as long as I could remember. Since Cyprus I'd been living in hell, flirting with the kind of mayhem and destruction only a hardcore drug addict will understand. All of the panic, the worthlessness, the agony, sorrow, depression, anger, sickness, the horror – heroin took it all away. The peace and comfort which heroin delivered scared the fuck out of me, and I knew then that my life would be over if I developed a heroin addiction. I'd come to terms with being an alcoholic. I'd come to terms with being a crack-head. But I knew that being a smack-head was something I could not live with. And I don't mean that I couldn't live with it because it would be awful. I mean I couldn't live with it because it would kill me. I knew this as sure as I know night follows day. Heroin was going to kill me.

Most addicts will tell you that their journey to recovery started when they reached rock bottom, whatever that might be. That might be when they lost their house, lost their kids or destroyed their relationship. Whatever the situation was, it would be a significant low point in their life. I'd already had so many rock bottom events in my life they were almost normal, but it was the high of heroin that made me see how low I could go. For me, my rock bottom was a high.

Puzzle piece 35

For James overcoming drugs and alcohol was difficult, when the praise wore off from music, people and all of the other substitutes, he became traumatic and depressed. Eager to fill the void within, even though James had undergone treatments and therapy, he was not ready to face the harsh effects of the real world.

The anxieties and stresses that triggered the original problems in James were still present. He believed if he indulged himself in one thing, that it would release the pressure. Taking heroin gave him the emotional response he desired; comfort.

CHAPTER 36.

STEP BY STEP

Recruiting a sponsor is part of the journey to recovery with AA and NA. While attending meetings, as they listen to the people speak about their addiction experiences, most addicts will meet someone whose story resonates with theirs. We pick up on how they achieved their sobriety, how their experiences and demons seem similar to our own, and we realise this person might be able to help us. When you find that person, it's a good idea to ask them to be your sponsor and help you through the 12-step programme.

My sponsor is someone we've met before. Adam was the bloke who first introduced me to AA – you'll remember I picked up Adam and his mates and drove them to the AA meeting, but was amazed that they were already totally pissed. While that particular AA meeting didn't go too well for me, I had since attended many others and heard Adam speak about his addiction and recovery journey, and his story struck a chord with me. He was as crazy and outrageous as I was but somehow managed to have fun while still being sober. I thought to myself, if he can do it, then so can I.

However, getting a sponsor isn't simply a case of asking someone. You'll need to show willingness and prove to them that you're ready to make the effort. Adam told me that he'd be my sponsor if I could stay sober for a couple of weeks and make a start on the AA 12-step programme. I was so desperate by this point that I promised him I'd do anything, whatever it takes, just point me in the right direction. "Just tell me what you want me to do and I'll do it," I said. And I meant it. By now I'd received the 'gift of desperation' and surrendered to the process. I was so ready for recovery. I'd decided I was going to put my heart and soul into it.

The first 90 days of sobriety are critical. It's the time when you'll be most aware of how your new life is vastly different from the one you had before. Your old 'drug-fuelled' routines will no longer be part of your life, so you'll need new routines to replace them. One of the new routines most people adopt is to attend fellowship meetings every day for those first 90 days. It's a commitment which adds structure and consistency and serves to fill the gaps left by your old daily routines. While most people commit to attending one meeting a day for those first 90 days, I was determined to double down and put everything I had into the recovery process. For those first critical 90 days I often went to two meetings each day, attending 120 in total. Like I said before, I'm an extreme-ist. Mine is a particularly strong strain of the disease and I don't do anything by halves.

In the meantime, Adam and I began working through the 'Big Book of AA'. It's a kind of handbook or guide which gives you the information, knowledge and tools you need to navigate through recovery to sobriety. For a whole week we sat down to read through the book, discussing how we might apply the principles and teaching points to our specific situations, before working through the accompanying worksheets.

The process was a revelation to me in more ways than one. The first revelation was that the information available in that book was enormously helpful. It was no wonder I had so much trouble staying clean and sober previously when I didn't even have the basic knowledge necessary to succeed. Initially I thought "If only I'd known this stuff sooner!" but, to be honest, even if someone had tied me down and force-fed it to me, I wouldn't have been ready to use it.

The other revelation I experienced as I worked through the book was about myself. A vital part of the recovery process is to deeply examine yourself, and that's something I'd ferociously avoided doing in the past. Looking at yourself critically and owning your mistakes and faults is a horrifically humbling thing to do, especially when you've been as fucked up and despicable in your life as I have. It's no wonder many people either simply can't or won't do the hard work involved. It's painful – excruciating even. But as I worked through the book with Adam, I could see how doing the hard work was going to be enormously important to my recovery success. You can't fix things if you can't understand how they're broken.

The 12-step programme is a progressive process which takes you deeper into recovery, with each step building on the progress achieved by those preceding it. The first step is to admit that we are powerless over alcohol and that our lives have become unmanageable. It's not an easy thing to do, but by the time you have secured someone to be a sponsor, you've probably reached this stage already. I certainly already knew I had a problem, that I was powerless to resist my addictions, and that alcohol was fucking up my life and everyone else's around me. Step one was already painfully evident in my case.

Step two is a little more difficult to absorb. In step two you have to accept that a power greater than ourselves could restore us to sanity. This step initially seemed a bit abstract to me, while also being a bit distasteful, because it seemed to insist that I start believing in God. My initial reaction had always been to fight against religion. I had no desire to be dictated to by some imaginary friend who got to tell me what I could and could not do. And, if there was a God, where the fuck had he been when I was fucking up my life and causing suffering to the people I loved? No, I wasn't going to become a fucking bible basher. If organised religion is your thing and you get some benefit from it, then good for you. I have nothing against that. It's just not for me.

Recognising these greater powers isn't easy when you've been as egotistical and violent as I have. I always felt like I could do whatever I liked and that nobody could stop me. As with many extreme-ists, I'd achieved things that most people would think impossible and, apart from the drink and drugs issue, I felt powerful enough. I'd seen no evidence of a God more powerful than me and so how could I believe this power could restore me to sanity?

Thankfully, there's a way for people like me to absorb the power of step two without signing up for church services. Indeed, it's pretty simple, when you get down to it. It's all about recognising that there are forces in this world which are more powerful than you are. Adam helped me to understand that greater powers do exist and that recognising this could help me enormously.

"Imagine you're standing on a beach watching the tide roll in, with wave after wave crashing on the shore," he said. "Now imagine you're trying to stop the waves from reaching the shore, pushing them back with all your enormous strength. Can you do it?"

"Of course not," I replied.

"See. There's a greater power," he smiled. And I saw that he was right.

From there we went over step two in detail to look at how a greater power works. My own personal greater power is the universe and the love that exists between me and my children. I can think of no greater power than this, and it was obvious to me how those powers have helped me in the past. It's indisputable that these powers have saved me from death and destruction on many occasions. These powers were things I could relate to and rely on in my time of need, to guide me toward making the right decisions, and to support me during my recovery process. I realised that I am not the great God of everything and that there is plenty of power greater than me. Knowing this helped me to let go of my ego and I realised I could ask for help when I needed it. I'd tried to get clean and sober on my own before, and failed. Help from someone or something more powerful than me would be necessary if I was to succeed this time.

It was a relief to me that I didn't have to believe in God or take up religion to become sober. Having let go of that problem, I removed a roadblock which was preventing me from benefiting from step two. I absolutely needed help from a power stronger than I was, and there were plenty of those to choose from. Adam, my sponsor, was a fabulous power which helped me through my recovery. The 12 steps were another greater power that I needed to help me succeed. There are so many greater powers you can't help but feel humbled, and that in itself is a giant step in the right direction.

Adam and I worked through the Big Book and the 12 steps in three months, exploring the philosophies, psychologies and practicalities of the process. And over that three months I underwent a significant psychic change – a spiritual awakening that changed how I perceived the world and altered what I thought and how I behaved. The process blew my mind and revealed so many things to me that it often felt like I was living in a completely different world. There were many tears, sometimes of despair and regret, but often they were tears of joy as if I'd been reborn in a brighter, happier, better reality.

Those 90 days removed my obsession to drink. I became totally driven by the idea of being clean and sober, knowing that there was a distinct possibility that I would never drink or use again. It was such a euphoric feeling that it gave me a calming, comforting sense of ease just like how I felt when I took heroin. I knew everything was going to be OK. I knew nothing could get me. I felt peaceful, content and happy for the first time in my life.

The first eight or twelve months of recovery are so very blissful. It's such a lovely experience, knowing you're going to be OK, seeing the world through fresh new eyes and realising the possibilities which lie ahead. It's often called 'the honeymoon period' and, like all honeymoons, it will come to an end.

Eventually, real life kicks in. And in real life you've lost your job, destroyed your family, spent all your money on drink and drugs, and you realise there's a long, long road ahead to the life you wish you could be living. Things aren't alright yet. You still have to live with the consequences of your addiction. You still have to live with your feelings. There's lots of work to be done. There are going to be problems along the way. And you'll still need to be constantly working on keeping your addiction at bay. Getting clean and sober isn't easy, but staying clean and sober is a million times easier than being an addict out there in the madness. This is the life you have ahead of you, and nothing about the recovery process is going to be quick or easy. I've learned that you have to question the value of anything which is quick and easy to achieve. If it's worth having, it's worth working for.

Thankfully, the 12-step programme teaches you how to live. It teaches you how to manage the stresses and problems that life will inevitably bring, except now you can deal with them without drugs or alcohol. The fact that the programme helps you stop drinking is great, but the real value is that it teaches you how to live life without being an addict. I think of it as a toolbox for maniacs.

Puzzle piece 36

James began to overcome his addiction in order to live a healthy life. There are different stages of recovery, James has passed the first stage of withdrawal and was now in the honeymoon stage.

Reaching this stage was a victory for James, he began to see his future brighter and brighter; free from drugs. However, it is advised not to be overconfident at this stage.

CHAPTER 37.

THE TEST

My sobriety day was June 1st 2017, and I haven't drunk alcohol or used drugs since. By the time this book is released in the summer of 2022, I'll have been sober and clean for over five years. Predictably, it hasn't all been plain sailing, but I certainly feel like a massive shift has happened and that I no longer feel so helplessly compelled to drink or take drugs. Of course, there are times when I feel like I want to drink, but I now have the knowledge, the tools and the strength to resist.

Since my sobriety day I have only once felt so helpless that I felt I would relapse. I was around six weeks clean at the time, during the hot summer days of 2017. I'd been out for a hike on Rivington Pike in Bolton and was returning home when I felt something click inside me, and I knew exactly what it was.

By the time I arrived home the disease was all over me. The sun was shining and I was hot and thirsty, a sensation I hadn't yet experienced since I'd been sober. All I could think of was sitting in my garden in the sunshine and cracking open a beer. The thought of it was glorious and every sense tingled with the anticipation of the sound, the taste, the smell, the feeling of drinking that ice-cold can. Once the thought was in my head it started to grow. It was all over me and wouldn't leave me alone. I tried to shake it, but I could think of nothing else. I was helplessly obsessed and I knew then that nothing could be done about it. I was, without a doubt, going to drink.

My mind was racing, flipping between the frantic desire to drink and the heartache I was about to cause the people who believed in me – the ones who had been there for me when I needed them most. I thought about my kids, about Kat, about Angela and Adam, and I thought about my poor mam who had endured so much suffering heartache because of me and my disease. I knew that if I started drinking and using again my disease would surely kill me, and that would destroy my mam too.

Instead of going straight home, I called into my mam's and told her I was sorry but I was going to drink and that I knew it would be the end. I was weak and hopeless. I told her I loved her and that I knew she had done all she could to help me, but I knew that nothing could help me now. We spent what seemed like forever talking, me trying to explain to her why I couldn't resist the demon, and her begging me to be strong and stay sober. Eventually, she persuaded me to call my sponsor, and even though I knew it would be useless, reluctantly, I agreed. I felt like I at least owed him an apology after all he'd been through and done for me, but I knew there was nothing he could do to stop me drinking. I'd decided I was going to thank him for his help and apologise for being a failure, and that I knew I couldn't be helped. Recovery just wasn't for me. I was an alcoholic. A drunk. An addict. I was one of the addicts which AA could not help. Thanks for all you've done for me, but I'm probably going to die.

I was sitting in my car ready to drive to the store to buy booze when I rang my sponsor, ready to tell him the score. The phone rang, and it rang, and it rang, and with each unanswered ring I felt more hopeless. When my sponsor didn't pick up I took it as a sign from the universe that I was meant to drink and, eventually, to die. It was a green light to give in to my addiction. I started the engine and headed for the store.

I was less than two minutes away when my sponsor rang me back. I stopped the car and stared at the screen until the ringing stopped. A second later it began to ring again, and right then, I knew I had a decision to make. I could ignore the phone and drink myself to death, or I could pick up and try to beat the demon that was raging inside me. It was a life-defining moment.

I picked up the phone and answered the call.

The next 24 hours were excruciating. We talk about higher powers a lot in recovery, but this was the first time I'd fully experienced a greater power at work. I had enough experience with the demon drink to know that there was no way back from where I was at that moment, so delirious and manic that nothing on earth could stop me drinking. I knew exactly how this would end because I'd been here so many times before, and each time it ended with me drunk, wasted, blacked out and back to being an addict. I'd tried to resist the urge before and failed. It would take something vastly more powerful than my earthly abilities to stop me from drinking.

My sponsor helped to save my life that day. He stayed with me while I screamed in agony and consoled me when I cried, knowing I was about to destroy my life once again. We worked through the 12 steps, and I followed his instructions, doing exactly what he told me to do. I accepted that I was helpless and I knew I needed his guidance if I was to beat this thing. So, I did what I was told.

That night I was still in pain so he suggested we go to an AA meeting. I didn't know what we would achieve by going, but I did as I was told. When we arrived I saw that there were around 40 people in the meeting, and I sat there tense and frantic, listening to people talk, while all the time still wanting to drink so badly. It was all over me, so badly I could hardly think. Eventually it was my turn to share, and I opened up, explaining what was happening, how I was crawling inside because I needed a drink so very much, sobbing as I explained the frantic situation I found myself in. I told them I had come to the meeting in the hope that I would find enough strength to get through the day without giving in to my addictions, but knowing it was helpless and that I knew I would give in and drink in the end.

By the time I'd finished speaking I felt a little better, but I knew I was still going to drink. As the next person shared their story, I sat with my head in my hands, creased up with the pain of the disease in my head. I listened to them talk and, in the back of my mind, I felt as if I recognised the voice of the person speaking, but was in too much pain to focus. They explained how they had been in exactly the situation I found myself today, how their sponsor brought them to a meeting in the depths of their despair, and how they had listened to the stories being shared and found strength enough to see out the day without drinking. They explained how the higher power was at work and spoke about the magic which was present during these meetings. Everything he said was so relevant to me it seemed as if he knew exactly who I was and what I needed to hear. And the more he spoke, the more I knew that I recognised the voice. Despite my pain and anguish, something was nagging away at me, trying to get in, and I couldn't help but think I needed to pay attention to whatever was going on.

When the meeting was over a few of us hung around to help clear away the chairs and, among them was the person who had shared the story which had been so relevant to me. He noticed me and came over and shook my hand, and it was then that I realised who he was. I can't tell you his name, but that person is one of the most famous sportspeople in the world. I understood what he was saying, and I realised I had options. I realised I didn't have to drink and that, with the help of the fellowship and the greater power, I could beat the demon that raged inside me. I knew I was going to be OK. Since that day I knew I would never again be that close to relapse. The obsession to drink had been lifted from me. I fought the demon and won. I'm not saying that meeting him is why I'm clean and sober today, but he certainly had a profound impact on me.

Less than a year later I was in a meeting, listening to a lad share his story. He was crying, explaining how he felt like he had to drink and that he fully expected to leave the meeting and get drunk as soon as possible. He explained that he hoped coming to a meeting might somehow, magically, stop him from drinking, but he didn't see how it would work. He'd resigned himself to being beaten down by the disease.

When he'd finished speaking, I began to speak to share my story from a year before when I'd been in exactly the same position he was in, and how hearing the story from the famous sportsman had turned my life around and kept me sober. I knew how he felt. I'd been where he was, and only listening to the sportsman's story had helped me to stop drinking. I told him that I hadn't seen the sportsman at any of the meetings I'd attended since that day a year ago, but I hoped I'd get the chance to thank him one day.

As I was talking to the struggling lad, telling him about my experience with the sportsman and how recovery was the new cool, I heard the door open and glanced to see who was entering. Guess who walked through the door? The fucking sportsman, I swear to God! He listened to me blathering on for a few seconds, registered what was happening, gave me a big grin and a thumbs up, before going to take a seat. "You're right," he said, looking in my direction as he shared his own story later in that meeting. "Recovery IS cool!" It was fucking surreal!

It's just one of the stories I tell when anyone questions that there's magic to be found at AA meetings. I know for a fact there is. I've experienced it first hand, and the fact that I'm still sober today is testament to it. The magic was passed on to me a year after I met with the sportsman, and it worked to keep me sober. I passed that magic on to the lad in the meeting that day, and he stayed sober too. The magic in AA meetings is a miracle, and I know exactly where I'd be without it. I've been tested many times since, but the magic is in me now and I know I can beat whatever the disease throws at me if I keep working on my recovery.

The secret to success is to keep working at it. Recovery is a journey, and the more you learn about it, the stronger your recovery will become. Don't forget, the disease is always growing and getting stronger too. If you want to stay ahead of it, you have to keep learning. You have to keep learning, growing stronger and digging deeper.

Puzzle piece 37

James had come to a positive point in his life and we wonder how one day his whole mood changed. The fear of relapsing would always linger over a recovering addict. It is possible that James associated the hot sun with memories of drinking with friends and having fun, stimulating the brain just like it once was.

It is possible the sun triggered his memory of the terrifying relapse in Cyprus. This is known as the traditional relapse, James debated making the conscious decision of whether or not to drink. However, he deterred his brain's instincts and overpowered the temptation.

CHAPTER 38.

DIGGING DEEPER

It took me 90 days to work through the AA's 12-step programme and I gave it everything I had. I completed all of the worksheets which accompany the programme, I attended 120 meetings and threw myself into every opportunity with which I could find ways to strengthen my recovery. The 12 steps aren't easy by any means, but they are instantly relatable to anyone who has battled with addiction. The process is achievable if you stick with it and put the effort in. You never really complete the 12 steps because learning about addiction is an ongoing process. The more you put into it, the more you get out of it.

Personally, I'd put everything I had into the 12 steps and my extreme-ist tendencies bit into the programme hard. I became obsessive about it and, for a time, there was nothing as important in my life. As I worked through the steps I began to feel like a new man, as if I was changing into the person I knew I should have been. I was changing into a better Shinny, one who wasn't a violent, abusive criminal. I was slowly changing into the me that I wanted to be.

While building a new me filled me with hope and delight, it seemed to have a different effect on Kat. I was changing, and so was my relationship with her. My new-found strength and sobriety meant

I was no longer the hard-man bad boy she'd fallen in love with, and I was no longer dependent on her for support either. It's a common experience for recovering addicts as the people around them find that they no longer recognise who they are any more. The transformation during recovery is so profound. It has to be. And as the addict changes, the people around them often stay the same.

Eventually, Kat couldn't take it anymore and she ended our relationship. While I was doing OK with my recovery I was still delicate and vulnerable, and splitting up with Kat sent me into a flat spin. The pain of rejection was so unbearable I can't describe it, and my disease seized the opportunity, latching onto my pain, just at the point where I thought I was winning.

Throughout my years as an addict I'd come to realise that being rejected breeds obsession in me. While this bloody-minded determination can be useful in some circumstances, such as when faced with a challenge, my obsession with Kat was entirely damaging. I became obsessed with getting her back and all of the compulsions and psychoses associated with my addiction raged inside me. My ego came charging back into my life, dictating my behaviour and driving me crazy all over again. While I wasn't actually drinking or using, I was behaving just as if I was. I became, in essence, a dry drunk. Despite all my 12-step work, I was soon having difficulty coping and I could see where I was headed. My disease was growing strong and I could feel it creeping closer, and I knew I needed to reinforce my recovery and take it up another level

I turned to my sponsor, the fellowships and the meetings and I begged them for help and, thankfully, they came through for me. They saved me on so many occasions during that time. They were there when I called them in the middle of the night, crying because I couldn't cope. They listened to me during the meetings and helped me through the hardest challenge to my sobriety that I had ever faced. And they guided me through the next stage of my recovery – the Narcotics Anonymous 12-step programme.

The AA's 12 steps had been a vital first stage, but the NA's 12 steps took me a whole lot deeper. The AA's worksheets totalled around a dozen pages of work and took 90 days to complete. The

NA's 12 steps were far more comprehensive, with my notes and workings filling four notepads. I worked every available minute of the day and night, but it still took over six months to finish the process. For many people, the process takes years.

The green and gold book called the Narcotics Anonymous Step Working Guide goes far deeper than the AA's 12 steps, digging into the deep, dark secret shit you really do not want to face. I know people who are still working through the steps years after they began the process. There are no shortcuts. If you do it properly, all the secrets you wish you never had to face will come to the fore, and there's nowhere to hide if you want to succeed.

Dedicating my time and energy to working through the green and gold book carried me through the devastating break up with Kat, not only giving me something to focus on, but also equipping me with the skills, tools and knowledge I needed to keep my recovery on track. Without the knowledge of self from that green and gold book I know I would have relapsed.

Puzzle piece 38

In James' early stages of recovery, he would have received a great deal of support. Most likely relying on Kat for this support. Throughout this journey, we are well aware of how vulnerable James really was, no matter what character he portrayed.

James was already trying to deal with the stress of his life as he adjusted to sobriety. This would have seemed to be too much for James. The rejection, stress and vulnerability all trigger bad memories. This led James to creep back into old coping strategies.

CHAPTER 39.

THE SHINNY SHOW

By the time you read this book I'll be five years sober and clean. I credit Alcoholics Anonymous and Narcotics Anonymous for equipping me with the tools to do the work I needed to do on myself to put addiction behind me. Today, I have choices. While I do still occasionally have the urge to drink, I am able to resist. That's a choice I did not have five years ago.

The journey to where I am today has not been an easy one. When I was balls-deep in my addiction I had no idea where to turn or who to ask for help. I stumbled around trying this and that, being defeated by failure and lack of knowledge at every turn. The recovery process has been long and hard, and much longer and harder than it needed to be, in my opinion. Looking back on what I have been through it's sad to think I could have avoided much of it if something like The Shinny Show had been around when I needed it.

The Shinny Show started as a way to springboard the Christmas Number One campaign. The song and the concept were formed around the idea that a bloke just out of detox could get his shit together enough to write and perform a song which reached Christmas number one. I would put out a video on Facebook every day telling people about the song and my progress through recovery.

From the very beginning, it was clear that I had hit on something which people found engaging. Some of them tuned in to listen to a crazy bastard with big ideas talk about how he was going to achieve the impossible and get a Christmas number one. Some tuned in for the feelgood factor, to watch someone who had turned their life around and attained a bit of notoriety. But many tuned in because The Shinny Show was one of the few places where addiction and alcoholism were being talked about openly. Sadly, talking about addiction isn't to everyone's liking.

One of the major principles of Alcoholics Anonymous and Narcotics Anonymous is the 'anonymous' part. It's a vitally important component of the programme as, without it, many addicts could not make it through the process without harming their family or their career. To this day I maintain that anonymity is central to the success of these fellowships and the programmes they promote. Unfortunately, some fellowship members take this secrecy too far and, instead, treat the fellowships like Fight Club. (If you haven't seen the film, just know that the first rule of Fight Club is that you don't talk about Fight Club. And the second rule of Fight Club is that you DO NOT talk about Fight Club.) Sadly, this approach does nothing to help the addicts and alcoholics who are frantically searching for help.

As the Christmas Number One campaign ended, I continued to post Facebook videos about my problems with drugs and alcohol, the highs and lows of my journey to recovery, my relapse, opening up honestly about each challenging and life-affirming stage. Anyone who knows me will tell you that I have got a bit of a big mouth, and as I've made these videos I haven't been shy about what's happened to me. As I got clean, people tuned in to cheer me on. As I relapsed, I broke their hearts, compelling them to tune in next time to see if I made it through the day. I'd sometimes do a show just minutes after returning home from a crack bender while everything was falling down around my ears. It was real and raw and entirely honest and authentic. It was like a reality TV show, but one with a message that, hopefully, could help others with their addiction challenges. As time went by, the show's audience grew and, at the same time, so did my commitment to help others with their recovery.

While I fully subscribe to the anonymity aspect of AA and NA, there's a huge gaping chasm of secrecy and hopelessness, into which many addicts fall when they can't find help. I've butted heads with many in the fellowship who have told me in no uncertain terms that I am going against the very principles of AA and NA by talking so openly about addiction. I call bullshit on that. As far as I am concerned, the secrecy extends only to the identities of the people undertaking the programmes, and the subject of addiction should not be at all taboo. Naming names and outing people would be wrong. In fact, it would be disgusting and I would never do that. But as far as talking about addiction and alcoholism is concerned, I'll be shouting from the rooftops for as long as I believe it will help those who need it. Just try stopping me.

You'll sometimes hear people say "If I can help just one person, then it'll be worth it." While helping one person is a fantastic thing to do, that's not how I work. I've never done anything moderately or on a small scale. You'll appreciate by now that I'm a go-large-or-go-home kinda guy. If I'm going to do recovery, I'm going to do it on as big a scale as possible. And if I'm going to help others, I want to help as many as I possibly can.

Step 12 of the AA's programme says:

"Having had a spiritual awakening as the result of these steps, we try to carry this message to alcoholics and to practice these principles in all our affairs."

To me, that gives me full permission to take the recovery message to other people. And, me being me, I feel the need to do that on a grand scale. As I worked through the 12-step programmes from AA and NA, it became clear to me that spreading the word was something I could do well. After all, I was not only committed as fuck towards recovery, but I also had a ready-made platform through which me and my big mouth could reach thousands of people. So I went for it big time and The Shinny Show was born. Fuck helping one person. I'm an extreme-ist. I want to help thousands!

Social media has been a fantastic tool to get the message of AA and NA out there to those people who have no other way of finding help. My show was one of the first to reach out on such a large scale and put this vital information out there. It was one of the few places where addiction and recovery were discussed openly and candidly, without shame or secrets. As we know and are taught in the 12-step programmes, secrets will keep you sick. The Shinny Show has blown the doors off the secrecy which once hid the fellowships from view. Now it's out there for anyone to see and we've helped countless people who might otherwise have suffered or died. We've provided support, knowledge, guidance and useful tools, not only for addicts but for their families and friends too. I realised I needed to recover out loud so that others didn't have to suffer in silence.

It's important to point out that The Shinny Show has helped me too. Doing the show has opened so many doors for me which have helped me to continue learning about addiction and recovery. As I've said before, everyone fighting addiction needs to stay ahead of the game in order to fight off the disease inside them. The disease doesn't get weaker the longer you remain sober. It's always growing, learning and getting stronger, so if you stand still, it'll eventually catch you and fuck you up. To keep fighting it effectively you have to keep learning and getting stronger yourself. The Shinny Show has enabled me to do exactly that, and we've brought thousands of other people on the recovery journey with us. For me, and for thousands of others, The Shinny Show is a forcefield against the evil of addiction. It gives us the strength to stay sober and enjoy a mayhem-free life.

As I said before, my journey to recovery has been too fucking long and too fucking hard. I don't want anyone to go through what I have been through, or at least no more than is absolutely necessary. My aim isn't to help people just give up alcohol or drugs. I want to go further than that. My hope is that people who have suffered from addiction can go on to live a pleasurable life.

I was kinda right back when I slagged off AA and NA for being cults. They kind of are really, but in a good way. That said, staying within the bubble of the addiction and recovery world isn't a good life to live. In an ideal world you'll be able to shrug off the label 'addict' and simply live a good life without drugs or alcohol. Spending your life identifying as an addict isn't healthy and if your entire identity is shackled to the fellowships or meetings that doesn't leave much room for pleasure. Yes, I understand that staying clean and sober needs consistent attention and constant learning, but there needs to be some life, some sparkle and enjoyment in there too. In the ideal world, you don't have to be just a 'recovering addict'. You can be so much more if you recover properly and fully.

My mission in life is to help you to do that. I hope my story, this book and the Shinny Show can help people to not only recover, but to thrive. We have a worldwide community to help and support anyone with addiction issues. We have experts and specialists from every corner of the recovery world, from doctors and therapists to celebrities and extreme-ists like you and I – and we're absolutely fucking determined to fight the fuck out of addiction, with you, side by side.

It's early January 2021 as I write the final chapters of this book, and the Prime Minister, Boris Johnson, has just initiated another full-scale national coronavirus lockdown. This pandemic has been a fucking disaster for everyone with addiction problems. Mental health issues, addictions and suicides have all gone through the roof in the last year, and this has been reflected in the number of people tuning in to The Shinny Show. Before the first lockdown we had 60,000 followers. By the time this book is released we expect to have somewhere near a quarter of a million.

The problem of addiction isn't going away.

I want The Shinny Show to be a big part of the solution.

Puzzle piece 39

The revolution of The Shinny Show became a completely different addiction for James. He was positive he could help as many people as he could and still does to this day. The Shinny Show promotes recovery and knowledge in hope that people find the page and achieve a life-changing experience.

James turned his disease and disorder into something completely positive to society. I believe James has become a better person by helping others. At the stage of his life where addiction was key, he was completely unaware of help. We now see this new person with new goals, not afraid to admit the defining points in his life.

CHAPTER 40.

Epilogue

Ask anyone who knows me and they will tell you that I should be dead by now. There is no logical explanation as to why I have survived, and so I can only conclude that there is indeed some greater power out there looking out for me. I don't know if it's a guardian angel, a God of some description, or simply some scientific, universal power that is configured in some way to keep me alive for some great, cosmic reason. Whatever it is, I know it exists and it has saved me from certain death on many, many occasions.

Through recovery I have come to realise and accept that living is indeed preferable to dying, and working through the 12-step programmes of AA and NA gave me the knowledge I needed to make a new life happen. And The Shinny Show has helped me to keep working at my recovery and provided me with an outlet for my extreme-ist compulsions. Helping others with their addictions gives me a purpose and something important and compelling to work towards. I can put everything into it and it gives my extreme-ism something productive to do.

However, despite being clean and sober, it hasn't all been a bed of roses. I didn't suddenly become a recovered addict and life was all peachy and rosy. I wasn't drinking or using any more, but for some months or years after I was still pretty fucked. Unlike my previous addiction fuelled world, where I had money and power and partied hard, demanding respect from everyone I met, my life was very different. For a start, I didn't have a job. There was no way I could have gone to work because the prospect of being put under any stress was terrifying. Instead I was claiming sickness benefits, and I was often so broke my mum would need to lend me money.

Not having a car was a huge problem for me. In the early days I was still too proud to catch a bus, even when alternative options were non-existent. I remember once speaking to my sponsor, explaining that I had to be somewhere but didn't have any transport to get me there. When he suggested I catch a bus, I scoffed and told him I'd never be seen dead on a fucking bus.

"Who the fuck do you think you are, Shinny?" he said. "You're not special. Getting on the bus is not below you. Plenty of people of all types use the bus, and you can too. To be honest, you ain't got many choices, so I'd just get on with it if I were you!"

And there, at that moment, I learned humility.

I also struggled financially until I sold my house. While the money from the sale came in handy, the real joy in selling that property was that I could put a dark chapter of my life behind me. That house was where I'd ruined my life. The amount of time I'd spent doing drugs, off my face and being violent in that house meant it would never be anything but a horrific reminder of the way I used to be. And all the time I still lived there, it would always be on my mind. I'd destroyed three families in that house and I needed a fresh, clean start. So, with the money from the sale, I rented a lovely apartment away from the places I'd frequented as an addict, and I also bought a nice new car. I could catch the bus if I had to, but I'd much rather have a car.

Yes, my new life without addiction has been very different and quite tough at times, but I don't want to go on too much about how tough it's been. I'm acutely aware that there are plenty of people in a much worse position than me. I meet addicts that are living on the street, and they're still coming to meetings, staying clean and making it as best they can. These people are the fucking superheroes, and I have it easy by comparison. But I also don't want to complain because it would do me no good to wallow in my reduced circumstances, comparing what I have now with what I had then. I realise I'm not that bloke anymore, and there's no comparison to be made. I'd much rather have what I have now, and that's the truth. I wouldn't swap this life for that one.

Most of my days since my sobriety day have been spent doing my best to get my recovery right. I spent every day trying to do more of the things I knew I should do and less of the things I knew I shouldn't. My old habits had to die, and to do that I needed to change the people and places where my old life lived. I became a bit of a recluse with my lifestyle revolving around meetings and recovery. I'm still friends with many of the people I knew when I was an addict. I haven't dumped them or ignored them, but I don't have much in common with them anymore. We don't hang out in the same places and get up to the same shit we used to. Many of them have grown up and moved on to better things, but some of them are still in the same place, doing the same stuff, and I don't want to be doing it with them anymore. Some have even paid attention to my recovery and come along on the journey with me.

I'm relieved to no longer be sitting in cafes and pubs, talking about shagging birds, getting into fights and drinking for fun. That's not how I have a good time anymore. My world is more attractive and interesting and fulfilling than that. It's often said in addiction circles that if drink and drugs are costing you more than money and you want it to stop, you'll need to change your playmates and your playgrounds. If you keep going back to the same old places, you'll inevitably keep going back to doing the same old things. Temptations are everywhere and old habits are so easy to slip back into. You must pull yourself out of the environments which are a catalyst for your addictive behaviour. After all, if you sit in a hairdresser's long enough you'll surely get a haircut eventually.

My family have seen changes too. My mam hasn't got her old son back, which is something many mothers of addicts wish for. Instead, my mam has got a new son, and we're yet to see how that will turn out. I'm still working out who I am and that project isn't finished yet. What I can tell you is that mam is delighted with the son she has today and is, as ever, one of my greatest supporters. I don't know what I did to earn her undying love and support given what I have put her through in the past, but I intend to pay her back and make her even more proud of me.

My kids have benefitted from the new me too. Their dad is stable, reliable, happy and helpful, at least most of the time anyway. It's how I wish my dad had been for me. When I was an addict, all I wanted in the whole world was to have my kids around me. I always thought that, if it was just me and the kids, the world would be wonderful. I laugh now, because most days, it is just me and the kids. They're here all the bloody time! I can't get rid of them! Be careful what you wish for, eh folks? Joking aside, my relationship with my kids has never been better and we love spending time together. Of course, there are the usual parenting challenges, but there is an underlying foundation of love that makes us a solid family. They know I'll always be there for them, no matter what. And that's something I couldn't promise when I was an addict. They don't have to worry about their dad anymore.

Even my sister, Gillian, is on my side now. She took much longer to come round and didn't trust me for such a long time. I had to prove myself to her and evolve enough to show her that I've changed for good. Today, she even comments on my Shinny Show page, telling me how proud she is of what I've done in my own life and how I'm helping others. She took some convincing, but I thank God for our connection.

And so we come to the end of the book, almost, and there's no easy way to wrap it up. Most stories have an end, but mine is still being written, and who knows what will happen next. It's typical for me to have a dozen crazy ideas a day and half a dozen projects on the go at any one time – this book being one of them. The Shinny Show on Facebook is growing so quickly it's taking on a life of its own. We've just launched Shinny's Socks, a step-by-step reminder encouraging those who are working through life's challenges. There's even a film in the pipeline, and after that who knows?

What I do know is that I'll still be here, thanks to the people I have around me and the help I have received from the AA and NA fellowships. When you've been as mental and as fucked up as I was it's hard to know what to do with yourself when you're free from your addiction and the destruction it brings. What am I, if I'm not an addict? Who am I? What do I want to be?

I know from bitter experience that I want to be the polar opposite of an addict.

I've grown to understand that the opposite of addiction is connection.

And that's what I have in abundance now.

Puzzle piece 40

By now we know James needed to substitute his addiction for something in order to avoid relapse. Supporting others certainly helped James identify himself in many ways. James had always struggled with this. Evidence suggests when you help others it can promote psychological changes in the brain linked with happiness. When we help others we make new friends and once again connect with our community. The sense of belonging reduced his loneliness, isolation and gave him purpose.

CHAPTER 41.

BULIMIA — MY MOST GUILTY SECRET

I've done some seriously fucked up shit in my time. I've lied, cheated and stolen. I've robbed people, hospitalised men, and deeply hurt the people I was supposed to love. I've been a violent alcoholic and a crack addict, and I've been able to talk openly and honestly about all of these topics. It's not been easy, but I've talked about it.

But one of my vices has been too humiliating for me to speak about, until now. One of my vices made me so guilty that I have continued to hide it, long after my alcoholism and drug addictions were in check. That secret, I am ashamed to admit, is bulimia.

I've always said that secrets will keep you sick, which is why I've freely admitted to all of the awful things I've done in my life. But even my mantra about secrets was not enough to make me face my most guilty secret of all. Admitting that I binge eat and then force myself to vomit the food back up was difficult to admit. Even talking about it now, I feel ashamed.

Perhaps it's because bulimia is often depicted as a 'women's issue', even though I can tell you that this is by no means a gender-specific problem. Thousands of men suffer from this affliction, especially nowadays when men are experiencing the same body-image discrimination that women have been subjected to for decades. As a man, admitting you have bulimia carries the same stigma as admitting that you like wearing women's clothing. Not that there's anything wrong with wearing women's clothing, but for egotistical men like me who are desperate to be respected and seen as powerful, admitting to such a feminine affliction goes against our very fibre. Hard drinking, drug-taking and sex could at least be considered 'macho' under some circumstances. Throwing up food so you can stay slim has no macho undertones whatsoever.

It's also difficult to explain why bulimia is so closely associated with addiction. To understand it you need to understand the mind of an addict. The first associated issue is our relationship with food and our compulsion to want more of anything which brings us pleasure or releases us from pain. The chapter in this book about food addiction explains the principle in detail, but it all boils down to the fact that anyone who is not comfortable in their own skin is looking for something to comfort them, something which eases the self-loathing. Eating food provides fulfilment, mouth-pleasure, a feeling of satisfaction that addicts find so very pleasurable, offering a similar temporary escape as that provided by drink and drugs. That's why so many former addicts end up creating unhealthy relationships with food, despite being clean of drink and drugs for many years. They substitute one pleasure-giving substance for another and ingest food to excess instead. It's another manifestation of extreme-ism.

I started throwing up food when I was 17. By that age I'd already been displaying extreme-ist tendencies, so I was a sitting duck for any pleasure-giving activity which could prey upon my insecurities and weaknesses. I'd heard from some of the bodybuilders I knew, that they ate 'bad' food for the pleasure of eating it, but threw it up afterwards so they didn't have to suffer the consequences. They could eat shit and still look good. "Wow!" I thought, "What a great idea!" If they could do it, so could I. I guess you could say I had some inspirational role models.

I remember going to the all-night petrol station and buying a bag full of goodies – Mars bars, chocolate biscuits, cakes – anything I thought would be relatively easy to puke up, knowing damned well that was exactly what I would be doing. I went back to my mum's and scoffed the lot, then I went into the bathroom to throw it all back up again. It was so easy to do that I just knew that I would do it again, and again, and again. And that's just what I did.

Since that day there has not been a month go by that I had not thrown up. I could last a few weeks of being strict with my diet and keep my compulsion at bay before I'd be back at the binge eating and vomiting-cycle. And it is a cycle. It preyed on the exact same insecurities which propelled my addiction. I felt like I was worthless, so I needed pleasure to dull the pain. I'd binge-eat to get that pleasure, then I'd feel worthless because I'd given in to my compulsions. Knowing that being fat would make my self-image matters worse, I'd throw up, which made me feel awful. And because I felt awful, I'd seek pleasure, and so I'd binge-eat.

Alongside this compulsive cycle also ran my need to be respected. The frightened, bullied child inside me needed my tough-man image to fend off the bullies. I needed to portray the image of a ferocious warrior to remain safe from the thing which terrified me more than anything. I needed to avoid being bullied and feeling worthless at all costs. I needed to be respected, and big bad bodybuilders always demanded respect. I knew my weakness for food could undo all of my good work, and if I turned into a fat slob I'd be prey for the bullies once again. In my head I imagined them rounding on me like a pack of hyenas and jackals, and I knew I must avoid that at any cost. I couldn't stop myself from eating, because I was weak, but I could avoid becoming a fat target for bullies if I threw it all up. It was a shitty solution, but for someone as weak as me, it seemed like the only option.

Underlying all of this was the addict's never-ending need for control. When you're weak and worthless, control over anything is a source of relief. Vomiting food was something I could have control over, and this gave me a tiny shred of self-worth and power. People who feel worthless will grasp at anything which they feel they can control, no matter how small, and the addict in us wants more of it. Even the retching became an attractive, kick-inducing activity which I still have some affection for, even today. We still crave control, even in recovery.

The effects bulimia had on me were almost as harmful as my addiction to drinking and drugs. Our relationship with food is such an important one and to mess up something so vital to life will inevitably do damage to our health. While inwardly I would be disgusted and ashamed, outwardly there are few signs of bulimia for people to pick up on. While the stomach bile I vomited would eventually rot away my teeth and gums, I was already suffering these symptoms because of my drink and drug abuse. Those close to us might catch on when they see us disappear to the bathroom after every meal. They may even hear you retching. Nevertheless, there's often little they can do about it. Many of the women that had been in my life had commented on the issue, only for me to tell them to "Shut the fuck up and fuck off". This was my thing and I wouldn't have them telling me what to do. I even had a mate from rugby take me to one side and tell me he was worried about me because he'd caught me throwing up. I just brushed him off, told him to forget it, that it wasn't a problem.

Honestly, I think all of the people who knew what I was doing had enough on their plate with the more dangerous aspects of my addiction. A bit of bulimia wasn't much of a worry when you can't moderate your drinking. Throwing up your dinner pales in significance compared with robbing people to pay for crack. The people around me turned a blind eye. It was just something else I did that was fucked up, and they had bigger things to worry about.

Of course, I knew people thought badly of me because of it. I knew they thought me weak, irresponsible and selfish. I knew this because that's exactly how I thought of myself. Such negative thinking and self-loathing is not only common in addicts, it's extreme. We don't like ourselves and we have no respect for who we are or what we do, so hurting ourselves is what we deserve, it's normal and it's appropriate. We hurt ourselves, harm our bodies, our minds, our relationships and our lifestyles because, why not? We're already a piece of shit, so what does it matter? We've already been weak and eaten food we know we shouldn't have, so throwing it up again is just another shitty thing to add to the list. Binge, feel shit, throw up, feel shit, eat again for the pleasure it brings – cycle and repeat. And, besides, it's not as bad as being fucked up on drink and drugs eh?

Perhaps all of these reasons I've listed above explain why I kept my bulimia secret for so long, even after my recovery from drink and drugs was well underway. It was a little naughty habit I could keep to myself – just a small one. It was my dirty little secret.

Bulimia was rarely a topic of conversation in the addiction therapy groups I attended. Their focus is, quite understandably, the specific issue the group was formed for – usually drink or drugs. The inclination to talk about associated afflictions, such as bulimia, is a distraction from the important work they do. Indeed, the doctrine of these groups is that, should you also suffer from other afflictions, you should find help to combat these too.

For me, I feel strongly that addiction and bulimia are interwoven, closely related and important to discuss together, on the same platform, in the same breath. Despite being clean and sober, deep down I knew I was still an addict, with the same uncontrollable urges manifesting in my behaviour as bulimia. Although I looked like I was winning, having stayed off drink and drugs, deep down I knew I was still losing. Bulimia was my secret, and it was keeping me sick. The embarrassment made me feel like I should hand in all of the medallions and keyrings I'd earned for staying clean and sober. Every time I vomited it felt like a relapse. I was in recovery, but I hadn't fully recovered. I was still failing.

Admittedly, it would have been a waste of everyone's time to attempt to address bulimia when I was still drinking and using. I had to face the most urgent problems first and solve those. I needed to solve the problems that were likely to kill me first. I had to build up my knowledge and understanding of addiction before I had enough conviction to tackle the bulimia – not because bulimia is worse or more difficult, but because the networks in place to help addicts are well established and vital for basic survival. I had to learn how to simply survive before I could learn how to be more healthy. Being sober and clean is just the beginning of a journey which can ultimately lead to personal development and self-mastery. It's a constant journey full of challenges and great rewards if you're willing to work at it.

There's a saying in the world of recovery that addicts put down the spoon (which is part of drug-use paraphernalia) and we pick up the fork, replacing our drug use with eating. It's an obvious transition for addicts who no longer get what they want from drink and drugs, but now find solace and pleasure in eating. It would be great if addicts could continue their journey of development by applying what they have learned to make the most of their potential. After all, let's not forget that those of us with extreme-ist tendencies have great potential if we use our extreme-ism as a force for good.

The good thing about being sober and clean is that you get your feelings back. Instead of blocking them out with drink and drugs, you get to feel pleasure, pain, love, security, disappointment and all of the other emotions that make life meaningful.

However, the bad thing is that you get your feelings back, including the shame, sorrow, regret, weaknesses and the understanding of all the things you've done in the past, and all the things you might do in the future. And often, people don't want to face those things, so they get themselves another addiction. But the truth will out, eventually. And then you'll invariably have to face your feelings, good and bad. Eventually, everyone has to own their demons. You can't have secrets. Your secrets will keep you sick.

I finally decided to face my bulimia demon during a session with a therapist. He took me through the work involved in unlocking and examining my past, bringing buried memories and experiences to the surface to be examined. Turns out my love affair with food developed from my loving relationship with my grandad, who would console me with food whenever I was upset or told off. It is only now after five years of recovery and work on myself, that I am in a position to understand and tackle these things. It's only since I have become well that I have the skills and the spiritual strength to face these associated issues. The more recovery work I do, the better able I become to deal with the shit from my past.

I admitted to myself that bulimia wasn't being kind to me. My knowledge and spiritual strength helped me to see it for what it is, to understand that throwing up wasn't doing me any good at all. For me, the whole recovery journey is about finding a way to be kind to yourself.

I know I'm still weak. I know that I'm susceptible to all of the demons which have plagued me in the past. But I also know that I'm not the same person anymore. I'm not the scared child, frightened of being bullied. That child has been forgiven for the wrongs he did. He was a child and didn't know any better. I've even forgiven myself for all of the atrocities I committed when I was an adult, because the person who did them was still a child too, and they knew no better either.

Since then I've grown. I've learned lots. I've worked hard to understand myself and the world around me. I have role models who have my best interests at heart. I know how to behave. I understand that how I think and the conversations I have with myself will affect my understanding of the world. It will dictate my behaviour, influence how those around me react, and ultimately, dictate how fulfilled and enriched my life can be.

As someone who has been there, my advice to you is to open up. Ask for the help you need. It's not weak to ask for help. You can't know everything. You are not the centre of the universe or the all-knowing. You are not the most powerful entity. You are flawed, and you will make mistakes. But you can learn. You can get better. And you can be forgiven too.

It's not just you. We're all stupid, crazy, flawed and fucked up in one way or another, and that's OK. We can work to manage the worst of ourselves and give the best parts a chance to shine, if only we can find a way to love ourselves.

I hope that me opening my big mouth to talk about these topics will offer someone a chance to face their own demons. I'm still the same mouthy, egotistical, extreme-ist Shinny I've always been, and that will never change.

Only now, I'm the version of Shinny that I can be (mostly) quite proud of.

Now it's your turn.

If I can do it, so can you.

MAKING OF AN ADDICT

Believe me, you're far, far stronger than you think.

Puzzle piece 41

Research shows that bulimia can be linked to psychological problems such as anxiety, PTSD and OCD. Bulimia can develop as a response to life changes and the cycle of bingeing and purging expresses this stress.

James' bulimia most likely stemmed from his childhood trauma and abuse of being overweight and quite obviously his low self-esteem. The continued search for respect and self-love is prominent in all of our lives.

James and every other recovering addict should be extremely proud of themselves for they have achieved what they thought was the impossible. Today we have the knowledge to become who we truly aspire to be.

You can and you will.

The End

Printed in Great Britain
by Amazon